FICTITIOUS AND SYMBOLIC
CREATURES IN ART

FICTITIOUS & SYMBOLIC CREATURES IN ART

WITH SPECIAL REFERENCE TO THEIR USE

IN BRITISH HERALDRY

By JOHN VINYCOMB

MEMBER OF THE ROYAL IRISH ACADEMY, FELLOW
OF THE ROYAL SOCIETY OF ANTIQUARIES OF IRE-
LAND, A VICE-PRESIDENT OF THE EX-LIBRIS SOCIETY

ST. GEORGE AND THE DRAGON

ILLUSTRATED

CHAPMAN AND HALL, LIMITED
11 HENRIETTA STREET, LONDON, W.C.

MCMVI

REPUBLISHED BY GALE RESEARCH COMPANY, BOOK TOWER, DETROIT, 1969

Library of Congress Catalog Card Number 76-89300

PREFACE

NDER the title of this book it is proposed to describe and illustrate only those fictitious and symbolic creatures which appear in British Heraldry. The list will include all those beings of whose existence we have not the direct evidence of our senses, and those exaggerations and combinations of natural forms which have been adopted in the system of symbolic heraldry handed down to us from the Middle Ages. Many of the ideas of the writers of that period were undoubtedly derived from still earlier sources, namely, classic story, sacred and legendary art, and the marvellous tales of early travellers ; others were the coinage of their own fancies and their fears.

As these unreal beings are constantly met with in symbolic art, of which heraldry is the chief exponent, it may be assumed that they have been adopted in each case with some obvious or latent meaning, as in the case of real animals ; they may, therefore, equally lay claim to our consideration as emblems or types, more especially as less attention has been devoted to them and the delineation of their forms by competent artists. The writer has been led into considering and investigating the subject with some degree of attention, from finding the frequent need of some reliable authority, both descriptive and artistic, such as would enable any one to depict with accuracy and true heraldic spirit the forms and features of these chimerical beings. Books of reference on heraldry unfortunately give but a meagre description of their shapes, with scarcely a hint as to their history or meaning, while the illustrations are usually stiff and awkward, representing a soulless state of art.

It cannot be said that artists at any period have succeeded, even in a remote degree, in embodying the highly wrought conceptions of the poets concerning these terrible creatures of the imagination. Milton seems to have carried poetic personification to its utmost limits. Who, for instance, could depict a being like this :

> " Black it stood as night,
> Fierce as ten furies, terrible as hell ! "

Out of the ambiguous and often conflicting accounts

of different authors and the vagaries of artists it became no easy task to arrive at a clear conception of many of the forms of these ideal monsters. The poet's pen may turn them to shapes, shadowy at the best; but the artist who follows the poet in endeavouring to realise and give tangible shape to these ideas finds it beyond his art to give material form and expression to his personifications with anything like photographic fidelity. Such shadowy beings prefer the dim light of allegory to the clear sunlight of reason, and shrink from closer inspection. Like all spectres they are ever most effective in the dark. In the childhood of the world, from the dawn of history, and all through the dim and credulous ages past, many such illusions have performed an important part in influencing the thought and lives of mankind. Over many lands these inherited ideas still exercise a paramount influence, but in the enlightenment of the coming time it is probable their power, like that of an evil dream, will fade entirely away with the dawn of a brighter day, and the memories of their name and influence alone remain. At present we are chiefly concerned with them as symbols, and with their mode of representation, breathing for a brief moment the breath of life into their old dead skins. These mythical creatures may be gazed upon, shorn of all their terrors, in the illustrations I have been enabled to make, and if it is found that from each creature I have not " plucked out the heart of its mystery " it is probably because there is no mystery whatever about it, only what to us now appears as an ingenious fiction engendered by a credulous, imaginative and superstitious past.   And so we find the old horrors and pleasing fictions, after figuring for ages as terrible or bright realities in the minds of entire peoples, reduced at length to the dead level of a figure of speech and a symbol merely.

J. VINYCOMB.

HOLYWOOD,
  COUNTY DOWN,
    April 1906.

CONTENTS

	PAGE
INTRODUCTION	I
NOTES ON ANIMATED BEINGS IN HERALDIC ART . .	13
THE SYMBOLISM OF ATTITUDE OR POSITION . .	18
THE HERALDIC SPIRIT—EFFECTIVE DECORATIVE QUALITY ESSENTIAL IN HERALDRY	22
CELESTIAL BEINGS	25
ANGELS	27
MISTAKEN MODERN CONCEPTION OF ANGELS . .	32
MEDIÆVAL ART TREATMENT OF ANGELS . . .	34
CHERUBIM AND SERAPHIM IN HERALDRY . . .	44
THE CHERUBIM AND SERAPHIM OF SCRIPTURE . .	47
EMBLEMS OF THE FOUR EVANGELISTS	53
CHIMERICAL CREATURES OF THE DRAGON AND SERPENT KIND	57
THE DRAGON	59
THE DRAGON IN CHRISTIAN ART	69
THE DRAGON IN THE ROYAL HERALDRY OF BRITAIN.	83
THE CROCODILE AS THE PROTOTYPE OF THE DRAGON	91
THE HERALDIC DRAGON	92
THE HYDRA	96
THE WYVERN	98
THE CHIMERA	102
THE LION-DRAGON	103
THE GORGON	103
THE COCKATRICE	104
BASILISK, OR AMPHYSIAN COCKATRICE	106
THE MYTHICAL SERPENT	108

PAGE

THE SCORPION 122
OTHER CHIMERICAL CREATURES AND HERALDIC BEASTS . 125
THE UNICORN 127
    MEDIÆVAL CONCEPTION OF THE UNICORN . . 130
      THE HORN OF THE UNICORN 133
THE PEGASUS 137
SAGITTARY, CENTAUR, SAGITTARIUS, CENTAURUS, HIPPO-
    CENTAUR 141
GRIFFIN OR GRYPHON 147
    THE MALE GRIFFIN 160
    OTHER VARIETIES OF THE GRIFFIN 161
THE OPINICUS, OR EPIMACUS 162
THE SPHYNX 163
THE PHŒNIX BIRD OF THE SUN 171
THE HARPY 179
THE HERALDIC PELICAN 182
THE MARTLET 186
THE ALERION 188
    THE LIVER (CORMORANT) 189
THE HERALDIC TIGRE OR TYGER 190
    THE ROYAL TIGER 193
LEOPARD, OR PANTHER, FELIS PARDUS, LYBBARDE . . 194
    THE PANTHER "INCENSED" 199
THE LYNX 203
CAT-A-MOUNTAIN—TIGER CAT OR WILD CAT . . . 205
THE SALAMANDER 209
HERALDIC ANTELOPE 213
THE HERALDIC IBEX 215
BAGWYN 216
THE CAMELOPARD, CAMEL-LEOPARD 216
MUSIMON, TITYRUS 217
THE ENFIELD 217
MANTIGER, MONTEGRE OR MANTICORA SATYRAL . . 218
    LAMIA OR EMIPUSA 220
    BAPHOMET 221

CONTENTS

PAGE

APRES 221
STELLIONES 221
FICTITIOUS CREATURES OF THE SEA 223
INTRODUCTORY NOTES 225
POSEIDON, OR NEPTUNE 237
MERMAN OR TRITON 239
THE MERMAID OR SIREN 243
THE SIRENS OF CLASSIC MYTHOLOGY 249
THE DOLPHIN OF LEGEND AND OF HERALDRY . . . 254
THE DAUPHIN OF FRANCE 265
THE HERALDIC DOLPHIN 267
THE SEA-HORSE 270
SEA-LION 274
SEA-DOG 275

LIST OF ILLUSTRATIONS

PAGE

CELESTIAL BEINGS :

Angel holding Shield 27
Egyptian Winged Deity 28
Hawk-headed and winged figure, emblem of Osiris . 29
Angel with Cloud Symbol 38
Angel Supporter 40
Kneeling Angel Supporter 41
Arms of the Abbey of St. Albans 42
Gloria in Excelsis Deo 43
Cherubs' Heads 44
A Seraph's Head 44
Arms—Azure a chevron argent between three cherubs'
    heads of the last 45
Cherubim and Seraphim of Scripture . . . 47
Angel crest of Tuite, Bart., co. Tipperary . . . 48
Tetramorph 52
Symbols of the Four Evangelists 54
The Lion of St. Mark, Venice 56

CHIMERICAL CREATURES OF THE DRAGON AND SERPENT KIND :

The Dragon 59
Japanese Dragon 65
Japanese Imperial Device 67
The Dragon of the Apocalypse 71
St. Michael and the Old Dragon 72
St. Margaret. From ancient carving . . . 73
St. George and the Dragon 74

CHIMERICAL CREATURES—*continued :*

Dragon Standard.   From the Bayeux Tapestry .   .   86
A Dragon passant   90
Crest, a Dragon's Head erased collared and chained   .   93
Arms of the City of London   94
Sinister supporter of the arms of Viscount Gough   .   95
Hercules and the Lernean Hydra.   From Greek vase .   96
The Hydra   97
A Wyvern holding a fleur-de-lis   98
A Wyvern, wings endorsed, tail nowed   .   .   .   99
Wyvern from the Garter plate of Sir John Gray,
    1436 A.D.   99
Wyvern, or Lindworm (German version)   .   .   . 100
Wyvern, wings displayed (early example)   .   .   . 101
Wyvern, wings depressed 101
Chimera, from a Greek coin   102
Cockatrice 105
Basilisk or Aphasian Cockatrice, tail nowed   .   . 107
Greek Shield, from painted vase in the British Museum 114
Brazen Serpent   114
Arms of Whitby Abbey 118
A Serpent, nowed, proper.   Crest of Cavendish .   . 121
Amphiptère, or flying Serpent 122
Scorpion   123
OTHER CHIMERICAL CREATURES AND HERALDIC BEASTS :
Unicorn salient   127
Crest, a Unicorn's Head, couped   128
The Legend of the Unicorn   131
Pegasus or Pegasos 137
Coins of Corinth and Syracuse 138
Pegasus salient   139
The Sagittary—Centaur 142
Ipotane, from Mandeville's travels   144
Compound figures, gold necklace   145
Centaur, Greek Sculpture   146

PAGE

OTHER CHIMERICAL CREATURES—*continued* :

A Griffin statant, wings endorsed 148
A Griffin passant, wings raised. (Early English) . . 149
A Griffin segreant, wings displayed. (German) . . 149
Sleeping Griffin 150
Griffin segreant (German version) 152
Gold Flying Griffin 154
Colossal Griffins, Burmah 155
Carved panel, a Griffin segreant 160
Male Griffin 161
Opinicus statant 162
Egyptian Sphynx 163
Theban, or Greek Sphynx 164
A Sphynx passant guardant, wings endorsed . . 170
The Phœnix 171
A Harpy, wings disclosed 179
The Harpy, Greek sculpture 180
A Harpy displayed and crowned (German version) . 181
Shield of Nüremberg 181
A Pelican in her piety, wings displayed . . . 182
Heraldic Pelican in her piety 183
Crest, a Pelican vulning herself proper, wings endorsed 184
The natural Pelican 186
The Martlet 186
Alerion displayed 188
Heraldic Eagle 188
An Heraldic Tigre passant 190
Supporter, an Heraldic Tigre, collared and lined . 191
Tigre and Mirror 193
A Leopard passant 195
A Leopard's Face, jessant-de-lis 196
Panther "Incensed" 200
The Lynx 203
Cat-a-Mountain saliant, collared and lined . . . 205
Crest, a Cat-a-Mountain, sejant, collared and lined . 206

PAGE

OTHER CHIMERICAL CREATURES—*continued :*

The crowned Salamander of Francis I. . . . 209

Salamander crest of James, Earl of Douglas . . 212

Heraldic Antelope 214

The Heraldic Ibex 215

Musimon, Tityrus 217

Mantygre, Satyral 218

Manticora. From ancient Bestiaria 219

Lamia. From old Bestiary 220

FICTITIOUS CREATURES OF THE SEA :

Poseidon. Dexter Supporter of Baron Hawke . . 237

Merman or Triton 240

Triton, with two tails (German) 240

Mermaid and Triton supporters 241

Mermaid 242, 243

Crest of Ellis 244

Die Ritter, of Nuremberg 245

Ulysses and the Sirens 249, 250

The Dolphin 254, 255

Dolphin of classic art 259

Coin of Ægina 262

Sign of the Dolphin 263

Banner of the Dolphin 265

Example—Dolphin embowed 267

Dolphin hauriant, urinant, naiant, torqued . . 268

Sea-horse naiant 270

Sea-horse erect 271

Arms of the city of Belfast 273

Sea-lion erect 275

Sea-dog rampant 276

INTRODUCTION

" Angels and ministers of grace defend us."—*" Hamlet."*

HE human mind has a passionate longing for knowledge even of things past comprehension. Where it cannot know, it will imagine ; what the mind conceives it will attempt to define. Are facts wanting, poetry steps in, and myth and song supply the void ; cave and forest, mountain and valley, lake and river, are theatres peopled by fancy, and

> " as imagination bodies forth
> The forms of things unknown, the poet's pen
> Turns them to shapes, and gives to airy nothing
> A local habitation and a name."

Traditions of unreal beings inhabit the air, and will not vanish be they ever so sternly commanded; from the misty records of antiquity and the relics of past greatness as seen sculptured in stupendous ruins on the banks of the Nile and the plains of Assyria, strange shapes look with their mute stony eyes upon a world that knows them but imperfectly, and

A

vainly attempts to unriddle the unfathomable mystery
of their being.   Western nations, with their growing
civilisations, conjured up monsters of benign or
baneful influence, or engrafted and expanded the
older ideas in a manner suited to their genius and
national characteristics.

The creatures of the imagination, "Gorgons and
Hydras and Chimeras dire," shapes lovely and shapes
terrible begot of unreason in the credulous minds of
the imaginative, the timid and the superstitious,—or
dreamy poetic fancies of fairies and elves of whom
poets sing so sweetly:

> "Shapes from the invisible world unearthly singing
> From out the middle air, from flowery nests
> And from the pillowy silkiness that rests
> Full in the speculation of the stars,—"
>
> KEATS.

> " or fairy elves,
> Whose midnight revels, by the forest side
> Or fountain, some belated peasant sees,
> Or dreams he sees,—"
>
> MILTON, *Paradise Lost*, Book i.

the nameless dreads and horrors of the unknown
powers of darkness, the pestiferous inhabitants of
wastes and desert places where loneliness reigns supreme, and imaginary terrors assault the traveller
on every hand, assuming forms more various and
more to be dreaded than aught of mortal birth,—
such vague and indefinable ideas, "legends fed by

time and chance," like rumours in the air, in the course of time assume tangible shape, receiving definite expression by the poet and artist until they become fixed in the popular mind as stern realities influencing the thoughts and habits of millions of people through successive generations. We see them in the rude fetish of the South Sea Islander, the myriad gods and monsters of heathen mythology, as well as in the superstitions of mediæval Europe, of which last the devil with horned brow, cloven hoofs and forked tail is the most " unreal mockery " of them all. The days of Diabolism and the old witch creed are, however, passed away ; but under the dominance of these ideas during centuries, in Protestant and Catholic lands alike, hundreds of thousands of innocent victims of all ages and both sexes were accused of the most absurd and impossible crimes, and subjected to almost inconceivable torture and death.

The dying Christian about to pass through the valley of the shadow of death, in the words of the poet, expresses his faith in the nearness of the spirit world :

> " I see a form ye cannot see
> I hear a voice ye cannot hear."

To the spiritually minded other forms, with more of the beautiful and less of the hideous and frightful, revealed themselves ; the solitary recluse, his body and mind reduced to an unnatural condition by fasting and penance, in mental hallucination beheld his celestial visitants with awe and adoration, and saw in visions angels and archangels, cherubim and seraphim towering in a blaze of glory to illimitable height and extremest space. The rapt seraph and the whole angelic host of heaven to his ecstatic gaze was a revelation and a reality as tangible as were the powers of darkness seen and felt by more sordid natures, incapable of the higher conceptions, and whose minds were accessible chiefly through their terrors.

To classic fable we are indebted for very many of the fictitious animals which heralds have introduced into coats armorial. In all ages man has sought to explain by myths certain phenomena of nature which he has been unable to account for in a more rational manner. *Earthquakes* were the awakening of the earth tortoise which carried the earth on its back; *the tides* were the pulses of the ocean; *lightning* was the breath of demons, the thunderbolt of Jupiter, the hammer of Thor; *volcanoes* were the forges of the infernal deities. In the old Norse legends we read of *waterspouts* being looked upon as sea serpents, and wonderful stories are related of their power and influence. The Chinese imagine *eclipses* to be caused by great dragons which seek to devour the sun. Innumerable beliefs cluster round the *sun, moon,* and *stars.* We may trace from our own language the extent of power which these peculiar beliefs have had over the human mind. We still speak of mad people as lunatics, gloomy people as saturnine, sprightly people we term mercurial; we say, " Ill-starr'd event,"

&c. &c. The ships of the early navigators, with masts and sails and other requisites for directing their motion or influencing their speed, would be objects of astonishment to the inhabitants of the countries they visited, causing them to be received with the utmost respect and veneration. The ship was taken for a living animal, and hence originated, some say, the fables of winged dragons, griffons, flying citadels, and men transformed into birds and fishes. The winged Pegasus was nothing but a ship with sails and hence was said to be the offspring of Neptune.

" In reality," says Southey, in his preface to the "Morte d'Arthur," vol. ii. 1817, "mythological and romantic tales are current among all savages of whom we have any full account ; for man has his intellectual as well as his bodily appetite, and these things are the food of his imagination and faith. They are found wherever there is language and discourse of reason; in other words, wherever there is man. And in similar states of society the fictions of different people will bear a corresponding resemblance, notwithstanding the differences of time and scene." And Sir Walter Scott, in his " Essay on Romance and Chivalry," following up the same idea, adds, " that the usual appearances and productions of nature offer to the fancy, in every part of the world, the same means of diversifying fictitious narrative by the introduction of prodigies. If in any romance we encounter the description of an elephant, we may reasonably conclude that a phenomenon unknown in Europe must have been borrowed from the East; but whoever has seen a serpent and a bird may easily aggravate the terrors of the former by conferring on a fictitious monster the wings of the latter ; and whoever has seen or heard of a wolf, or lion and an eagle, may, by a similar exercise of invention, imagine a griffon or a hippogriff."

Beyond the common experiences of every-day life the popular mind everywhere cares very little about simple commonplace practical truths. Human nature seems to crave mystery, to be fond of riddles and the marvellous, and doubtless it was ever so and provided for in all the old faiths of the world.

" The multitude of dragons, diverse as they are, reflecting the fears and fancies of the most different races, it is more than probable is a relic of the early serpent-worship which, according to Mr. Fergusson, is of such remote antiquity that the religion of the Jews was modern in comparison, the curse laid on the serpent being, in fact, levelled at the ancient superstition which it was intended to supersede. Notwithstanding the various forms under which we find the old dragon he ever retains something of the serpent about him, if no more than the scales. In the mediæval devil, too, the tail reveals his descent." (Louis F. Day.)

The fictitious beings used as symbols in heraldry may be divided into two classes : (1) Celestial beings mentioned in Holy Writ, and those creatures of the imagination which, from the earliest ages, have held possession of men's minds, profound symbols unlike anything in the heavens or in the earth beneath or in the waters under the earth. They may be abstract ideas embodied in tangible shape, such as the terrible creature, the type of some divine quality, that stands calm, immovable, and imperishable within the walls of our National Museum; such forms as the dragon, of the purely imaginative class, and those creatures compounded of parts of different real animals, yet unlike any one of them, each possessing special symbolic attributes, according to the traditional ideas held concerning them. (2) Animals purely heraldic, such as the heraldic tiger, panther incensed, heraldic antelope, &c., owe their origin and significance to other ideas, and must be accounted for on other grounds, namely, the mistaken ideas resulting from imperfect knowledge of these objects in natural history by early writers and herald painters, to whom they were no doubt real animals with natural qualities, and, as such, according to their knowledge, they depicted them ; and although more light has been thrown upon the study of natural history since their time, and many of their conceptions have been proved to be erroneous, the well-known heraldic shapes of many of these *lusus naturæ* are still retained in modern armory. These animals were such as they could have little chance of seeing, and they probably accepted their descriptions from " travellers' tales," always full of the marvellous— and the misleading histories of still earlier writers.

Pliny and many of the writers of his day describe certain animals in a way that appears the absurdest fable ; even the lion described by him is in some points most unnatural. Xenophon, for instance, describing a boar hunt, gravely tells us : " So hot are the boar's tusks when he is just dead that if a person lays hairs upon them the hairs will shrivel up ; and when the boar is alive they—that is, the tusks— are actually red hot when he is irritated, for otherwise he would not singe the tips of the dogs' hair when he misses a blow at their bodies." The salamander in flames, of frequent occurrence in heraldry, is of this class. Like the toad, " ugly and venomous," the salamander was regarded by the ancients with the utmost horror and aversion. It was accredited with wondrous qualities, and the very sight of it "abominable and fearful to behold." Elian, Nicander, Dioscorides and Pliny all agree in that it possessed the power of immediately extinguishing any fire into which it was put, and that it would even rush at or charge the flame, which it well knew how to extinguish. It was believed that its bite was certainly mortal, that anything touched by its saliva became poisonous, nay, that if it crept over a tree all the fruit became deleterious. Even Bacon believed in it. Quoth he : " The salamander liveth in the fire and hath the power to extinguish it." There is, too, a lingering popular belief that if a fire has been burning for seven years there will be a salamander produced from it. Such is the monstrous character given to

one of the most harmless of little creatures: the
only basis of truth for all this superstructure of fable
is the fact that it exudes an acrid watery humour
from its skin when alarmed or in pain.

Spenser, in the "Fairy Queen," Book i, cant. v. 18,
according to the mistaken notions of his time, compares the dangerous dissimulation and treacherous
tears of Duessa (or Falsehood) to the crocodile :

> " As when a weary traveller that strays
> By muddy shore of broad seven-mouthed Nile,
> Unweeting of the perilous wand'ring ways,
> Doth meet a cruel, crafty crocodile,
> Which in false guise hiding his harmful guile,
> Doth weep full sore, and shedding tender tears ;
> The foolish man, that pities all the while
> His mournful plight, is swallowed unawares
> Forgetful of his own that minds another's cares."

And Shakespeare, *2 Henry VI.* iii. 1 :

> " as the mournful crocodile
> With sorrow snares relenting passengers."

Quarles, too, in his " Emblems " :

> " O what a crocodilian world is this,
> Compos'd of treach'ries and insnaring wiles ! "

Bossewell, an heraldic writer of the sixteenth century, after the model of his forerunner, Gerard Leigh,
edified his readers with comments on natural history
in such a delightful manner (according to his friend
Roscarrocke) as to provoke the envy of Pliny in

Elysium, though now these descriptions in many instances only serve to call up a smile from their very absurdity. With "veracious" histories of this description, is it to be wondered at that such beings as those referred to were made use of in heraldry and accepted as types or emblems of some particular quality in man? As an instance of how an error in the form of an animal may be perpetuated unperceived, it may be mentioned that even in the best books on heraldry, natural history, and in other illustrated publications, the elephant is rarely to be seen correctly delineated. A peculiarity in his formation is that the hind legs bend in the same manner as the fore legs, so that, unlike other quadrupeds, it can kneel and rest on its four knees, whereas it is usually depicted with the hind legs to bend in the same way as those of the horse or the cow. When artists and herald-painters continue to commit this blunder unobserved, some palliation may be afforded to the old heralds for their offences against zoology in the errors and delusions arising from lack of information. They could have little opportunity of acquiring a correct knowledge of the rarer kinds of animals; they had not the advantage of seeing menageries of wild beasts, or of consulting books on natural history with excellent illustrations, as the modern herald may do. Only when their scanty information fell short did they venture to draw on their imaginations for their beasts, after the manner of an ancient worthy, who " where the lion's skin fell short, eked it out with the fox's."

Some writers, however, maintain that these monstrosities are not so much the result of ignorance of the real forms of the beasts as that they were intended to typify certain extraordinary qualities, and therefore exaggeration of the natural shapes and functions was needful to express such qualities. This may be true in some instances. Under this idea the noble form of the lion may have been distorted to resemble the wild cat in the fury of its contortions. *The Panther incensed*, breathing fire and smoke out of its mouth, nose and ears, seems as if taken from some misleading history—like that of the boar, by Xenophon, already referred to—or the result of the erroneous description of some terrified traveller. This is a natural and probable mode of accounting for its unnatural appearance. It may, however, fairly be said that the natural ferocity of the brute, and also its destructive qualities, are most fitly typified by the devouring flame issuing from the head of this bloodthirsty and treacherous beast of prey.

The Heraldic Pelican, again, is evidently a mistake of the early artists, similar to the heraldic tiger, heraldic antelope, &c., and the persistent following of the traditional " pattern " by the heralds when once established. Early Christian painters always represented this emblem of devoted self-sacrifice, *A Pelican in her piety*—that is, feeding her young with her own blood —as having the head and beak of an eagle or bird of prey such as they must have believed it to possess, and with which it would be possible that it could lacerate its own breast ; and not with the clumsy and ungainly "bill" peculiar to this species of bird, which we know is more suited to gobble up small reptiles than to "*vulning*" itself.

Some symbols, again, are neither real nor do they pretend to be fabulous, such as the *two-headed eagle*, but are pure heraldic inventions that have each their special signification. *The tricorporate lion* lays no claim to be other than the symbol of a powerful triune body under one guiding head ; the *three legs conjoined*—the arms of the Isle of Man—is an old Greek sign for expedition. Many other instances will, no doubt, occur to the reader of similar emblems of this class.

Notes on Animated Beings in Heraldic Art

Notes on Animated Beings in Heraldic Art

" One chief source of illustration is to be found in the
most brilliant, and in its power on character, hitherto
the most effective of the Arts—HERALDRY."

RUSKIN,
" Relation of Wise Art and Wise Science."

ERALDRY is *par excellence* the
science of symbols. A pictorial de-
vice is subject to no exact or regular
law, provided it carries its meaning
with it. Heraldry, on the contrary,
insists on the observance of certain
definite and easily understood rules constituting it
a science, by the observance of which any one
acquainted with heraldic language may, from a concise written description (or *blazon* as it is termed),
reconstruct at any time the symbol or series of symbols intended, and with perfect accuracy ; for a
heraldic emblem once adopted remains unchangeable,
no matter with what amount of naturalness or con-
ventionality it may be done, or with what quaintness

or even grotesqueness it may be treated ; the symbol remains intact. "*A lion rampant*," "*a dragon*," or any other heraldic figure is, therefore, a fixed and immutable idea, and not to be confounded with any other, no matter what the style of artistic or decorative treatment it may receive.

Notwithstanding the evident intention everywhere in heraldry to be symbolic, in attitude as well as in tinctures, we find the greatest errors and absurdities constantly perpetrated. To many it seems as if it was not considered essential to acquire a knowledge of the rudiments of the science. Heraldry is a living language, and when the attempt is made to express it without proper knowledge the result can only be unmitigated nonsense. By inattention to those principles which regulate the *attitude*, the *tinctures*, and the disposition of every part of an armorial achievement, discredit is brought upon the subject, which should fall upon the head of the ignorant designer alone. No matter what heraldic position of an animal may be blazoned (though it admits of only one interpretation), we find the most unwarrantable latitude frequently taken by otherwise skilful artists in depicting it. The designer becomes a law unto himself, and it is posed and treated in a way to suit the fancy of the moment. A lion is only a lion to him, and it is nothing more. To the true herald it is very much more. As a mild instance, see the unkind treatment meted out to the supporters of the Royal Arms. The lion and unicorn are both "rampant," and the head of the lion is turned towards the spectator (termed *guardant*). Not content to be represented in the regulation positions, they will be found depicted in most strange and fantastic attitudes not recognised in heraldry—not supporting or guarding the shield, which is their special function. At the head of the *Times* newspaper they are represented playing at hide and seek round the shield; elsewhere we see them capering and prancing, or we find them sitting, like begging dogs, as if ashamed of themselves and their vocation.

I may here quote from a most admirable work : "That the decorative beauty of heraldry, far from being that of form and colour alone, was also an imaginative one depending much on the symbolic meaning of its designs, there can be no doubt. . . . Early Christian Art was full of symbols, whose use and meaning were discussed in treatises from the second century onwards. By the eleventh it had become systemised and ranged under various heads,— Bestiaria for beasts, Volucaria for birds, and Lapidaria for stones. It permeated the whole life of the people in its religious uses, and entered romantically into the half-religious, half-mystical observances of chivalry, the very armour of the valiant knight being full of meanings which it was his duty to know." *

* "Decorative Heraldry," by G. W. Eve.

B

The Symbolism of Attitude or Position

It must be evident to every one who has given any thought to the subject that a definite idea is meant to be conveyed to the mind by the attitude in which an animal is depicted ; and such figures are not mere arbitrary signs, like the letters of the alphabet, which of themselves convey no meaning whatever. "*A lion rampant*" is, as the term suggests, a lion in the act of fighting, rearing on his hind legs to meet his antagonist. He is therefore depicted with wildly tossed mane, staring eyes, and *guly* mouth ; his muscular limbs and distended claws braced up for the combat betoken the energy and power of the noble brute. How different is the idea conveyed by the lion *statant* in the firm majesty of his pose, calmly looking before him ; or *couchant*, fit emblem of restful vigilance and conscious power, prepared on the instant alike to attack or defend.

Should any reasons be needed to enforce the necessity of adhering strictly to the heraldic law in which attitude plays such an important part, it may be needful only to refer to one or two examples, and cite as an instance in point the noblest of all created beings, and ask whether, of the many acts in which imperious man himself may be heraldically portrayed, the action or position in which he is to be depicted should not indicate distinctly the idea that is to be associated with the representation? whether vauntingly, like the old kings,—

"with high exacting look
Sceptred and globed"

—attributes of his power,—or as a bishop or saint in the act of benediction,—kneeling in prayer as on mediæval seals,—the three savage men *ambulant* on the shield of Viscount Halifax,—or the dead men strewn over the field on the seal of the city of Lichfield—in each the primary idea is *man*, but how different the signification! It will therefore be understood that the particular action or posture, or any of the various forms in which real or imaginary creatures may be blazoned in heraldry, gives the keynote to its interpretation, which, in this respect, is nothing if not symbolic.

It will be seen that to interpret the meaning implied in any particular charge, the *tinctures*, as well as the *attitude*, must be considered. These, taken in combination with the *qualities* or *attributes* we associate with the creature represented, indicate in a threefold manner the complete idea or phase of meaning intended to be conveyed by the composition, and may be thus formulated :

(1) THE CREATURE.—The primary idea in the symbol is in the particular being represented, whether real or fictitious, as *a man, a lion, an eagle, a dragon,* &c., of the form and accepted character for some particular quality or attri-

bute of mind or body, as *fierceness*, *valour*, *fleetness*, &c.

(2) ATTITUDE.—The various attitudes or positions in which it may be depicted in heraldry, each denoting some special meaning, as *rampant, sejant, dormant,* &c.

(3) TINCTURE.—Whether blazoned *proper* (that is, according to nature) or of some of the heraldic tinctures, as *or* (gold), *gules* (red), *azure, vert,* &c., each tincture, according to the old heralds, bearing a particular and special signification.

Tinctures in armorial devices were, however, not always introduced on these scientific principles or adopted from any symbolic meaning, but as arbitrary variations of colour for distinction merely, and as being in themselves equally honourable; colour alone in many instances serving to distinguish the arms of many families that would otherwise be the same. Hence the necessity for accuracy in blazoning.

Guillam lays down some general rules regarding tne symbolic meaning by which all sorts of creatures borne in arms or ensigns are to be interpreted, and by which alone a consistent system can be regulated. "They must," he says, "be interpreted in the best sense, that is, according to their most generous and noble qualities, and so to the greatest honour of their bearers. . . . The *fox* is full of wit, and withal given wholly to filching for his prey. If, then, this be the charge of an escutcheon, we must conceive the quality represented to be his wit and cunning, but not his pilfering and stealing ; " and so of other beasts. Even in wild and ruthless animals and fictitious creatures, symbolic heraldry delights in setting forth their most commendable qualities, as fierceness and courage in overcoming enemies, though they may also possess most detestable qualities.

In like manner all sorts of peaceable or gentle-natured creatures must be set forth in their most noble and kindly action, each in its disposition and that which is most agreeable to nature, rather than of an opposite character. Heraldic art thus stamps a peculiar note of dignity for some particular respect in the emblematic figures it accepts, as for some special use, quality or action in the thing depicted ; and this dignity or nobility may have a twofold relation, one betwixt creatures of divers kinds, as *a lion* or *a stag*, *a wolf* and *a lamb ;* the other between beings of one and the same kind, according to their various attitudes or positions in which they may be represented, as a stag *courant* or *at speed*, and a stag *lodged* or *at bay ;* a lion *rampant* and a lion *coward*—one will keep the field, the other seek safety in flight, just as one attitude conveys a different signification from another.

The Heraldic Spirit—Effective decorative Quality essential in Heraldry

IT will be observable that in the hands of a capable designer imbued with the true heraldic spirit, all objects, animate and inanimate, conform after their kind to decorative necessities, and assume shapes more or less conventional, and, as far as is consistent with effective display of the charge, are made to accommodate themselves to the space they must occupy. Fierce and savage beasts are made to look full of energy and angry power, while gentle-natured creatures are made to retain their harmless traits. In a monster of the dragon tribe, strong leathern wings add to his terrors; his jaws are wide, his claws are strong and sharp; he is clothed in impenetrable armour of plates and scales, his breath is fire and flame, lightning darts from his eyes, he lashes his tail in fury; and all the while the artist is most careful so to spread the creature out on shield or banner that all his powers shall be displayed at once.

Whatever liberty the artist may take in his interpretation of the form of bird, beast, or monster, there is, however, a limit to his licence beyond which he may not go. He may not alter the recognised symbolic attitude, nor change the tincture; he is scarcely at liberty to add a feature. He may curl the mane of his lion, fancifully develop its tongue and tail, and display its claws in a manner for which there is little or no authority in nature ; but if he add wings, or endow it with a plurality of heads or tails, it instantly becomes another creature and a totally different symbol.* A wise reticence in treatment is more to be commended than such fanciful extravagance.

The early artists and heralds, in their strivings to exaggerate in a conventional manner the characteristics of animals for their most effective display, appear to have reached the limits of which their art was capable, and important lessons may be gained from their works. With the extended knowledge of natural history, and the advanced state of art at the present day, decorative and symbolic heraldry should take a leading place in the twentieth century, as in the words of Ruskin, it has been "hitherto the most brilliant" and "most effective of the Arts."

* The above notes on heraldic treatment are largely adapted from the admirable works on Decorative Art, by Louis F. Day.

Celestial Beings

Angels

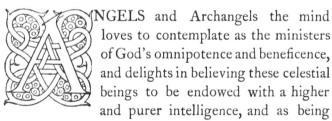

"_They boast etherear vigour and are form'd_
From seeds of heavenly birth."—VIRGIL.

"_Down hither prone in flight_
He speeds, and through the vast ethereal sky
Sails between world and world with steady wings :
Now on the polar wind, then with quick fan
Winnows the buxom air."—MILTON.

NGELS and Archangels the mind
loves to contemplate as the ministers
of God's omnipotence and beneficence,
and delights in believing these celestial
beings to be endowed with a higher
and purer intelligence, and as being
nearer to the divine nature.   In all ages civilised man
has thought of them and represented them in art as of

form like to his own, and with attributes of volition and power suggested by wings. Scripture itself justifies the similitude ; the Almighty is sublimely represented as " walking upon the wings of the wind." Wings have always been the symbol or attribute of

Egyptian Winged Deity.

volition, of *mind*, or of the *spirit* or *air*. No apter emblem could be found for a rapid and resistless element than birds or the wings of birds; and however incongruous such appendages may be, and anatomically impossible, it is figuratively as the messengers of God's will to man that we have come to view these celestial habitants.

The idea of adding wings to the human form has existed from remote antiquity, and for the earliest suggestion of celestial beings of the winged human type we must look to the art works of Egypt and Assyria. In Egyptian art, Neith, the goddess of the heavens, was sometimes represented with wings, and in the marbles of Nineveh we find human figures displaying four wings.* In classic art wings are

* See Audsley's " Glossary of Architecture," " Angel," p. 101.

given to certain divinities and genii. The Jews probably borrowed the idea from the Egyptians, and the early Christians adopted—in this as in many other instances — existing ideas in their symbolical art to express the attribute of swiftness and power, and the sanction of the practice doubtless fixed it for acceptance through all future epochs of Christian Art.

In holy writ and Jewish tradition angels are usually spoken of as men, and their wings appear to be implied rather than expressed, as when Abraham in the plains of Mamré addresses his celestial visitors as " my lord," when Jacob wrestles

Hawk-headed and winged figure, emblem of Osiris, which, having of all birds the most piercing eye and the most rapid flight, serves to express the divine intelligence and activity. (Palace of Nimrod in the Louvre.)

with the angel, and more particularly when the Angel at the Sepulchre is described by St. Matthew, "His countenance was like the lightning and his raiment white as snow," and by St. Mark as " A young man clothed in a long white garment."

The Seraphim and Cherubim as winged beings are more perfectly described in the Scriptures.

The Wings Variously Coloured.—Not content with a simple departure in form from all natural wings, the early and Middle Age artists resorted to many expedients to invest their angels' wings with unearthly characteristics. Colour was a fertile field for their ingenuity, and they lavished all their brilliant hues in accentuating or separating the several orders of feathers comprising the wings; now rivalling the rainbow, now applying the startling contrasts of the most gorgeous tropical butterfly ; at other times sprinkling or tipping the richly painted feathers with burnished gold, or making them appear alive with brilliant eyes.

Vesture.—In Early Christian Art the white vesture spoken of by St. Matthew and St. John, almost invariably adopted, consisted of garments resembling the classic tunica and pallium, sometimes bound with the "golden girdle " of Revelation. During the mediæval period they were clad in every brilliant colour. Angels do not often appear in the works of art executed during the first six centuries of the Church; and previous to the fifth century they were invariably represented without the nimbus—that attribute of divinity with which they were almost always invested throughout the whole range of Middle Age art.

Nimbus.—The nimbi given to all the orders of the angelic hierarchy are circular in form, with their fields either plain or covered with numerous radiating lines or rays, sometimes with broad borders of ornament, but never with the *tri-radiate* form, which was specially reserved for the persons of the trinity.

Lord Bacon ("Advancement of Learning," Book i.) says we find, as far as credit is to be given to the ecclesiastical hierarchy of the supposed Dionysius, the Senator of Athens, that the first place or degree is given to the angels of love, which are termed *Seraphim*; the second to the angels of light, which are termed *Cherubim*; and the third, and so following places, to thrones, principalities, and the rest, which are all angels of power and ministry, so that the angels of knowledge and illumination are placed before the angels of office and domination.

Fallen Angels.—We learn from Tradition that many angels, originally holy like the rest, fell from their pristine purity, becoming so transformed in character that all their powers are now used for the purpose of doing evil instead of doing good. These are to be identified with the devils so frequently mentioned in holy writ. By the artists of the Middle Ages they are depicted in as hideous a manner as could be conceived, more generally of the Satyr form with horns and hoofs and tail, which last connects them with the Dragon of the Apocalypse, the impersonation of the Supreme Spirit of evil (*see* Dragon). In Milton's conception Satan—the fallen Angel—assumes noble and magnificent proportions.

Mistaken Modern Conception of Angels

MANY poets and artists of modern times appear to have lost sight of the traditions of sacred art, and in their endeavours to spiritualise the character of angelic beings have in this respect been led to portray them as altogether feminine in form and appearance. This error should be carefully avoided, because in a spiritual as well as in a human sense the vigorous active principle they represent, besides having the warrant of Scripture, is more fitly represented by man than by woman.

Mahomet, who borrowed his ideas mostly from the Christians, in this instance, possibly to guard his followers from some latent form of idolatry, said of angels with some show of reason, that " they were too pure in nature to admit of sex," but to meet the ideas of his followers he invented another race of celestial beings for the delight and solace of the faithful in the paradise to which he lured them.

Ministering Spirits or Guardian Angels.—These form a frequent theme of poets and artists. The idea was apparently evolved from the mention of " ministering spirits" before the throne of God in holy writ, and from the ecclesiastical legends and traditions of the Christian mythology of early date, derived from still earlier sources. Thus Milton speaks of—

" one of the Seven
Who in God's presence, nearest to the throne
Stand ready at command, and are his eyes
That run thro' all the heavens, and down to earth
Bear his swift errands."

Paradise Lost, iii.

According to ancient Jewish belief, each person had his or her guardian angel, and a spirit could assume the aspect of some visible being :

" But she constantly affirmed that it was even so.
Then said they, 'It is *his angel.*' "

Acts xii. 15.

" Brutus as you know was Cæsar's *Angel :*
Judge, O ye God, how dearly Cæsar loved him."

SHAKESPEARE, *Julius Cæsar*, Act iii. sc. 2.

Spenser finely expresses the idea of the good and evil influences continually warring unseen about us, and his gratitude for the effective protection of the guardian spirits :

" How oft do they their silver bowers leave,
To come to succour us that succour want !
How oft do they with golden pinions cleave
The flitting skies, like flying pursuivant,
Against fowle fiends to ayde us militant !
They for us fight, they watch, and dewly ward,
And their bright squadrons round about us plant ;
And all for love, and nothing for reward :
O why should heavenly God to men have such
regard ?

C

Milton beautifully assumes the pure nature of saintly chastity attended by ministering spirits :

> " A thousand liveried angels lackey her,
> Driving far off each thing of sin and guilt,
> And in clear dream and solemn vision,
> Tell her of things that no gross ear can hear ;
> Till oft converse with heavenly habitants
> Begins to cast a beam on the outward shape."
>
> " Comus."

And Scott, in figurative language, apostrophising woman in her higher and more spiritual sphere, says in " Marmion " :

> " When pain and anguish wring the brow,
> A ministering angel thou ! "

Shakespeare expresses a prevailing idea that the pure in heart will become ministering angels in heaven ; Laertes, at the grave of Ophelia, fiercely thunders forth :

> " I tell thee, churlish priest,
> A ministering angel shall my sister be
> When thou liest howling."

Mediæval Art Treatment of Angels

ACCORDING to ecclesiastical legend and tradition there are nine degrees of angelic beings. St. Dionysius relates that there are three hierarchies of angels and three orders in each ; and by wise allegories each had his special mission, and they were each depicted with certain insignia by which they were recognised in art representations, which vary somewhat in examples of different periods.

The nine choirs of angels are classed as follow, with the name of the chief of each, according to ancient legend :

Cherubim	Jophiel	*Dominions*	Zadchiel	*Principalities*	Camiel
Seraphim	Uriel	*Virtues*	Haniel	*Archangels*	Michael
Thrones	Zaphkiel	*Powers*	Raphael	*Angels*	Gabriel

According to A. Welby Pugin's "Glossary of Architectural Ornament and Costume," and other authorities, we learn the mediæval conception of these beings.

The following emblems are borne by angels : FLAMING SWORDS, denoting " the wrath of God "; TRUMPETS, "the voice of God "; SCEPTRES, "the power of God " ; THURIBLES, or censers, the incense being the prayers of saints ; INSTRUMENTS OF MUSIC, to denote their felicity.

The APPARELS, or borders of their robes, are jewelled with SAPPHIRE for "celestial contemplation"; RUBY, "divine love"; CRYSTAL, "purity"; EMERALD, "unfading youth."

ARCHANGELS are the principal or chief angels, and are extraordinary ambassadors. Among these the name of GABRIEL—the angel of the annunciation, the head of the entire celestial hierarchy—denotes "the power of God"; MICHAEL, "who is like God "; RAPHAEL, "the healing of God " ; URIEL, " the fire of God."

ANGEL is the name, not of an order of beings, but of an office, and means messenger : wherefore angels are represented YOUNG to show their continued strength, and WINGED to show their unweariedness ; WITHOUT SANDALS, for they do not belong to the earth ; and GIRT, to show their readiness to go forth and execute the will of God. Their garments are either WHITE, to denote their purity, or GOLDEN, to show their sanctity and glory, or they are of any of the symbolical colours used in Christian Art.

A writer in the *Ecclesiastical Art Review*, May 1878, I. Lewis André, architect, says that "we seldom find angels clad in any other ecclesiastical vestments than the ALB (or tunic of various colours), and the amice. The AMICE is sometimes like a mere loose collar ; at other times it has richly embroidered APPARELS (or borders), and is exactly like the priestly vestment as worn in the Middle Ages. Instead of the amice we sometimes find a scarf or cloth tied in a knot around the neck, the ends falling down in front.

" In Anne of Brittany's prayer-book is a beautiful figure of St. Michael. He has a rayed nimbus, a cross on a circlet round his head, a richly embroidered *dalmatic* (a long robe with sleeves partly open at the sides), and holds a sword in his left hand. The emblems of St. Michael are a crown, a sword, a shield charged with a cross of St. George, or a spear with the banner of the cross, or else with scales in his hand.

Sometimes, as at South Leigh, Oxon., he is in complete armour.

"The archangels are often figured with a trumpet in the right hand, scarfs round neck and loins; six wings, sometimes four at the shoulders and two at the hips, the legs bare from the thighs. The four archangels are frequently represented in complete armour and with swords.

"The angels in the Benedictional of St. Ethelwold nearly resemble much later representations; they have wings and the nimbus or aureole, long hair and girded loins, whilst the feet are bare, as is generally the case at all periods of Gothic Art; but the characteristic drapery is loose and flowing as in the Saxon figures of saints; the wings are short and broad, the nimbus is generally rayed like the spokes of a wheel (a form seen in the work of Giotto, with whom it seems to have been a favourite). The alb or vesture has loose sleeves, and at times a mantle or cope envelops the figure; both sleeves and mantles have embroideries or apparels."

"The modern taste," says the same writer, "for giving angels pure white vesture does not appear to be derived from the Middle Ages, and certainly not from the best period when angels were clad in every brilliant colour, as a beautiful example at St. Michael's, York, shows. Here an angel swinging a golden censer has a green tunic covered with a white cloak or mantle. The nimbus is bright blue, and the wings have the upper parts yellow, and are tipped

with green.   At Goodnestowe church, St. Michael
has a deep crimson tunic, a white mantle edged with
a rich gold border, green wings, and a light crimson
nimbus,"and mention is here made of the white vesture
of the angel at the Sepulchre, and that nowhere else
does the Gospel mention any
angel clad in white but in
the narratives of Our Lord's
resurrection.

Angel with Cloud Symbol.

" Often the angels' wings
are feathered red and blue
alternately, as on the pulpit
at Cheddar, Somerset. Sometimes the wings have feathers
like those of a peacock, on the
Chapter House, Westmin-
ster; round the Wall Arcade,
angels have their wings inscribed with a text on every
feather.   This corresponds
with the French 'hours' of
Anne of Brittany, where an
angel (St. Gabriel) wears a mantle with a text running
along the border."

It was not uncommon to represent angels in carving and stained glass in the latter part of the fifteenth
century as feathered all over like birds.

Cloud Symbol of the " Sky" *or* " Air."—Artists of the
Mediæval and Renaissance periods, following classical
authority, employed the cloud symbol of the sky or

air in their allegories and sacred pictures of divine
persons, saints, and martyrs, to denote their divine or
celestial condition, as distinguished from beings "of the
earth—earthy." The adoption of *the little cloud* underneath the feet, when the figure is not represented flying,
naturally suggested itself as the most fitting emblem
for a support, and avoided the apparent incongruity of
beings in material human shape *standing* upon *nothing*.
The suggestion of the aerial support here entirely
obviates any thought of the outrage on the laws of
gravity.

Another distinguishing attribute is the Nimbus
—an emblem of divine power and glory—placed
behind or over the head. The crown is an insignia
of civil power borne by the laity ; the nimbus is
ecclesiastical and religious. The pagans were familiar with the use of the nimbus, which appears upon
the coins of some of the Roman Emperors. It was
widely adopted by the Early Christian artists, and up
till the fifteenth century was represented as a circular
disc or plate behind the head, of gold or of various
colours, and, according to the shape and ornamenta-
tion of the nimbus, the elevation or the divine degree
of the person was denoted. It was displayed behind
the heads of the Persons of the Trinity and of angels.
It is also worn as a mark of honour and distinction
by saints and martyrs. At a later period, when the
traditions of early art were to some extent laid aside,
i.e., from the fifteenth century until towards the end
of the seventeenth century, as M. Dideron informs us,

a simple unadorned ring, termed a "circle of glory,"
"takes the place of the nimbus and is represented
as hovering over the head.   It became thus idealised
and transparent, showing an outer circle only; the
field or disc is altogether omitted or suppressed, being

drawn in perspective and
formed by a simple
thread of light as in the
Disputer of Raphael.
Sometimes it is only an
uncertain wavering line
resembling a circle of
light.   On the other
hand, the circular line
often disappears as if
it were unworthy to
enclose the divine light
emanating from the
head.   It is a shadow of
flame, circular in form
but not permitting itself
to be circumscribed."

Angel Supporter.

Although the forms of angels are of such frequent
occurrence in Mediæval Art they seem to abound
more especially in the fifteenth century.   Angels
are seen in every possible combination, with ecclesiastical and domestic architecture, and form the
subject of many allusions in heraldry.   They are frequently used as supporters.

Charles Boutell, M.A., "English Heraldry,"

p. 247, says, regarding angels used as supporters to the armorial shield: "The introduction of angelic figures which might have the appearance of acting as 'guardian angels' in their care of shields of arms, was in accordance with the feelings of the early days of English heraldry ; and, while it took a part in leading the way to the systematic use of regular supporters, it served to show the high esteem and honour in which armorial insignia were held by our ancestors in those ages." And reference is made to examples sculptured in the noble timber roof of Westminster Hall and elsewhere. As an example we give the shield of arms of the Abbey of St. Albans.

Kneeling Angel Supporter.

Figures of angels holding shields of arms, each figure having a shield in front of its breast, are frequently sculptured in Gothic churches. They appear on seals, as on that of Henry of Lancaster about 1350, which has the figure of an angel on each side of it. The shield of Richard II. at Westminster Hall, bearing the arms of France ancient and England quarterly, is supported by angels, which, if not rather ornamental than heraldic, were possibly intended to denote his claim to the crown of France, being the supporters of the Royal arms of that kingdom.   Upon his Great Seal other supporters are used. There are also instances of the shield of Henry VI. being supported by angels, but they are by some authorities considered as purely religious symbols rather than heraldic.

Arms of the Abbey of St. Albans.

The supporters of the King of France were two angels standing on clouds, all proper, vested with taberts of the arms, the dexter France, the sinister Navarre, each holding a banner of the same arms affixed to a tilting-spear, and the *cri de guerre* or motto, " Mont-joye et St. Denis."   The shield bears the impaled arms of France and Navarre with several orders of knighthood, helmet, mantling and other accessories, all with a pavilion mantle.

Although Francis II., Charles IX., Henry III. and IV. and Louis XIII. had special supporters of their arms, yet they did not exclude the two angels of Charles VI., which were considered as the ordinary supporters of the kingdom of France.   Louis XIV., Louis XV. and Louis XVI. never used any others.

Verstegan quaintly says that Egbert was "chiefly moved" to call his kingdom England "in respect of Pope Gregory changing the name of Engelisce into Angellyke," and this "may have moved our kings upon their best gold coins to set the image of an angel." *

" . . . Shake the bags
Of hoarding abbots ;
    their imprisoned *angels*
Set them at liberty."
          SHAKESPEARE,
          King John, iii. 3.

The gold coin was named from the fact that on one side of it was a representation of the archangel in conflict with the dragon (Rev. xii. 7). The reverse had a ship. It was intro-

duced into England by Edward IV. in 1456. Between his reign and that of Charles I. it varied in value from 6*s*. 8*d*. to 10*s*.

* "Restit. of Decayed Intell. in Antiq." p. 147.

Cherubim and Seraphim in Heraldry

" On cherubim and seraphim
Full royally he rode."
STEENHOLD.

" What, always dreaming over heavenly things,
Like angel heads *in stone with pigeon wings."*
COWPER, " Conversation."

IN heraldry A CHERUB (plural Cherubim) is always represented as the head of an infant between a pair of wings, usually termed a " cherub's head."

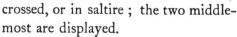

Cherubs' Heads.

A SERAPH (plural Seraphim), in like manner, is always depicted as the head of a child, but with three pairs of wings; the two uppermost and the two lowermost are contrarily crossed, or in saltire ; the two middlemost are displayed.

A Seraph's Head.

Clavering, of Callaby Castle, Northumberland, bears for crest a cherub's head with wings erect.   Motto : CŒLOS VOLENS.

On funereal achievements, setting forth the rank

and circumstance of the deceased, it is usual to place over the lozenge-shaped shield containing arms of a woman, whether spinster, wife, or widow, a cherub's head, and knots or bows of ribbon in place of crests, helmets, or its mantlings, which, according to heraldic law, cannot be borne by any woman, sovereign princesses only excepted.

In representing the cherubim by infants' winged heads, the early painters meant them to be emblematic of a pure spirit glowing with love and intelligence, the head the seat of the soul, and the wings attribute of swiftness and spirit alone retained.

Arms—Azure a chevron argent between three cherubs' heads of the last.

The body or limbs of the cherub and seraph are never shown in heraldry, for what reason it is difficult to say, unless it be from the ambiguity of the descriptions in the sacred writings and consequent difficulty of representing them. The heralds adopted the figure of speech termed synecdoche, which adopts a part to represent the whole.

Sir Joshua Reynolds has embodied the modern conception in his exquisite painting of cherubs' heads, *Portrait Studies of Frances Isabella Ker, daughter of Lord William Gordon*, now in the National Collection. It represents five infants' heads with wings, in different positions, floating among clouds. This idea of the cherub seems to have found ready acceptance with poets and painters. Shakespeare sings :

> "Look how the floor of heaven
> Is thick inlaid with patines of bright gold :
> There's not the smallest orb which thou beholdest
> But in his motion like an angel sings,
> Still quiring to the young-eyed cherubim—
> Such harmony is in immortal souls :
> But while this muddy vesture of decay
> Doth grossly close it in, we cannot hear it."

Many of the painters of the period of the Renaissance represented the cherub similarly to those in Reynolds' picture. They were also in the habit of introducing into their pictures of sacred subjects nude youthful winged figures, " celestial loves," sporting in clouds around the principal figure or figures, or assisting in some act that is being done. Thus Spenser invests "The Queen of Beauty and of Love the Mother" with a troop of these little loves, " Cupid, their elder brother."

> " And all about her neck and shoulders flew
> A flock of little loves, and sports and joys
> With nimble wings of gold and purple hue ;
> Whose shapes seemed not like to terrestrial boys,
> But like to angels playing heavenly toys."
> *Faerie Queen*, Book x. cant. x. p. 153.

These must not, however, be confounded with the cherub and seraph of Scripture. It was a thoroughly

pagan idea, borrowed from classic mythology, and
unworthy of Christian Art. It soon degenerated
into "earthly loves" and "cupids," or amorini as
they were termed and as we now understand them.

Cherubim & Seraphim of Scripture

In Ecclesiastical Art literal renderings of the descriptions contained in the Old Testament and the
Apocalypse are not of unfrequent use. A more
lengthened reference to these great Hebrew symbolic
beings will not be considered out of place, as there is
great doubt and uncertainty as to their forms.

These mystic symbolic beings were familiar to all
the patriarchs—from Adam, who gazed upon them in
Paradise, and against whom on his expulsion they
stood with flaming sword, turning every way to bar his
return—to Moses, who trembled before it on Mount
Sinai ; while to the Priests and Levites, the custodians
of the Ark of the Covenant in the Tabernacle, the

cherubim remained the sacred guardians in the Holy of Holies of the palladium of the national faith and liberties during the brightest and, as it has been termed, the most heroic period of Jewish history.

Josephus, the more effectually to excite respect for the great Hebrew symbol in the minds of his readers, purposely throws over it the veil of obscurity. He says : " The cherubim are winged creatures, but the form of them does not resemble that of any living creature seen by man." In the works of Philo Judæus there is an express dissertation upon the cherubim. The learned Brochart and many others have attempted to elucidate the subject to little purpose. The ambiguity which always accompanies a written description of objects with which we are imperfectly acquainted applies with greater force to this mysterious being combining so many apparently conflicting attributes.

Angel crest of Tuite, Bart.
co. Tip.

To the prophetic vision of Ezekiel, the description of which, in the opinion of competent critics, excels in grandeur of idea and energy of expression the most celebrated writers of ancient and modern times, the reader is referred, as it supplies at first hand almost all that can be known concerning the fearful form of the cherubim.

The four living creatures that support the throne of God exhibited to Ezekiel a fourfold aspect; they had each the face of *a man*, the face of *a lion*, and the face of *an ox*; they also had the face of *an eagle*. They had each four wings; they had the hands of a man under their wings. " Two wings of every one were joined one to the other, and two covered their bodies." They were accompanied by wheels which " went upon their four sides, and they turned not when they went "; " and their whole body, and their backs, and their hands, and their wings, and their wheels were full of eyes "; " and the living creatures ran and returned as the appearance of a flash of lightning." Such is a concise description of their appearance as set forth in Ezekiel (chap. i.).

" This wonderful and mysterious hieroglyph must be considered as a striking and expressive emblem of the guardian vigilance of providence, all-seeing and omniscient; while the number of wings exhibit to us direct symbols of that powerful, that all-pervading spirit which, while it darts through nature at a glance, is everywhere present to protect and defend us " (Dideron).

So attached were the Jews to this celestial symbol that when Solomon erected that stupendous temple which continued the glory and boast of the Hebrew nation for so many ages, we are told (1 Kings, vi. 29, viii. 6, 7), he carved all the walls of the house

D

round about with the sculptured figures of the cherubim, and on each side of the ark was a cherub of gold plated upon olive wood fifteen feet high, with their faces to the light, their expanded wings embracing the whole space of the sacred enclosure, serving as a visible sign or symbol of God's immediate presence, whence the saying of David, " God sitteth between the cherubim" (Ps. xcix. 1). In this place God perpetually resided in the form of a bright cloud or shining luminous body, termed " shechinah," whence the divine oracles were audibly delivered.

Milton gives the following description of the Seraph Raphael :

> " At once on the eastern cliff of Paradise
>   He lights, and to his proper shape returns
>   A seraph wing'd ; six wings he wore to shade
>   His lineaments divine ; the pair that clad
>   Each shoulder broad came mantling o'er his breast
>   With regal ornament : the middle pair
>   Girt like a starry zone his waist, and round
>   Skirted his loins and thighs with downy gold
>   And colours dipped in heaven ; the third, his feet
>   Shadows from either heel with feather'd mail
>   Sky tinctured grain.   Like Maia's son he stood
>   And shook his plumes, that heavenly fragrance fill'd
>   The circuit wide."
>   *Paradise Lost*, Book v.

The *cherub* is traditionally regarded as a celestial spirit which in the hierarchy is placed next in order to the seraphim. All the several descriptions which the Scripture gives us of cherubim differ from one another, as they are described in the shapes of men, eagles, oxen, lions, and in a composition of all these figures put together. The hieroglyphical representations in the embroidery upon the curtains of the tabernacle were called by Moses (Ex. xxvi. 1) " cherubim of cunning work " (Calmet).

The *seraphim* are regarded as an order of angels distinguished for fervent zeal and religious ardour. The word means " burning," *i.e.*, with Divine Love.

The seraphim are described by Isaiah (vi. 1–3): " I saw also the Lord sitting upon a throne, high and lifted up, and his train filled the temple. Above it stood the seraphim : each one had six wings ; with twain he covered his face, and with twain he covered his feet, and with twain he did fly. And one cried to another and said, Holy, Holy, Holy, is the Lord of Hosts : the whole earth is full of his glory." And in Revelation (iv. 6) : " Round about the throne were four beasts full of eyes before and behind, and the first beast was like a lion, and the second beast like a calf, and the third beast had a face as a man, and the fourth beast was like a flying eagle. And the four beasts had each of them six wings about him, and they were full of eyes within." It will be noticed that these descriptions differ from that of Ezekiel, not only in the number of wings, but also in the individuality of each beast being separate and independent, not compounded of the four.

Several forms of these mystical creatures, says Audsley, have been devised by the early mediæval artists ; those which display the entire forms of *the man, the lion, the ox,* and *the eagle,* all winged and invested with the nimbus, appear to have been most frequently made use of. They are to be met with formed of the *heads of the mystical creatures* on bodies or half-bodies of *winged human figures ;* at other times we find them comprised in the heads and wings only of the four symbolic creatures. Sometimes they are found united and forming one mysterious being called the *Tetramorph* with four heads and numerous wings covered with eyes, the feet resting on wheels, which are also winged. The example is taken from a Byzantine mosaic in the convent of Vatopedi, on Mount Athos.

Tetramorph.

Pugin's " Glossary of Ecclesiastical Ornament and Costume " says the cherubim are frequently represented of a bright red colour to set forth the intensity of divine love, and usually standing upon wheels, in reference to the vision of the prophet Ezekiel.

Cherubim and seraphim seem always vested in the
alb or tunic, and a scarf tied in a knot round the
neck.

Emblems of the Four Evangelists

THE winged living figures, symbols of the evangelists, which are most frequently met with, and which
have ever been most in favour with Early Christian
artists, appear to have been used at a very early date.
They are taken from the vision of Ezekiel and the
Revelation of St. John. "The writings of St. Jerome,"
says Audsley, " in the beginning of the fifth century
gave to artists authority for the appropriation of the
four creatures to the evangelists," and for reasons
which are there given at length.

ST. MATTHEW : *Winged Man*, Incarnation.—To
St. Matthew was given the creature in human like-
ness, because he commences his gospel with the
human generation of Christ, and because in his
writings the human nature of Our Lord is more
dwelt upon than the divine.

ST. MARK : *Winged Lion*, The Resurrection.—*The
Lion* was the symbol of St. Mark, who opens his
gospel with the mission of John the Baptist, " the
voice of one crying in the wilderness." He also sets
forth the royal dignity of Christ and dwells upon His
power manifested in the resurrection from the dead.
The lion was accepted in early times as a symbol of

the resurrection because the young lion was believed always to be born dead, but was awakened to vitality by the breath, the tongue, and roaring of its sire.

St. Luke : *Winged Ox*, Passion.—The form of the ox, the beast of sacrifice, fitly sets forth the sacred office, and also the atonement for sin by blood, on which, in his gospel, he particularly dwells.

St. John : *The Eagle*, Ascension.—The eagle was allotted to St. John because, as the eagle soars towards heaven, he soared in spirit upwards to the heaven of heavens to bring back to earth revelation of sublime and awful mysteries.

Independently of their reference to the four evangelists these figures sometimes refer to *the Incarnation*, *the Passion*, *the Resurrection*, and *the Ascension*.

Sedulius, a priest and poet of the fifth century, says much the same in the following verse :

Hoc Matthæus agens, Hominem generaliter implet:
Marcus ut alta fremit box per deserta Leonis:
Jura sacerdotis Lucas tenet ore Jubenci:
More bolens Aquilæ berbo petit astra Johannes.

The Lion of St. Mark.—In the ninth century the rapidly rising State of Venice was dignified by the reception of the relics of St. Mark, transported thither from Alexandria. " Few patron saints," says Theodore A. Buckley, " enjoy a greater popularity, whether socially or locally exemplified. His lion was emblazoned on the standard of the Republic, and stamped on the current coins, while his name was identified with the pride, the power, and glory of all Venice." *

Emblems of the evangelists do not often appear in heraldry.

* " Great Cities of the Middle Ages."

Walter Reynolds, Archbishop of Canterbury, according to a manuscript at Lambeth (executed for Archbishop Laud), bore *azure on a cross or, between the symbols of the evangelists of the last, four lions rampant gules.*

The Freemasons appear to use a similar coat of arms upon their seal, viz., *a cross between the emblems of the four evangelists, and for supporters two cherubims, all proper.*

The Lion of St. Mark, Venice.

Chimerical Creatures of the Dragon and Serpent kind

The Dragon

*" The scaly monster of a dragon, coiled
Full in the central field—unspeakable,
With eyes oblique retorted, that askant
Shot gleaming fire."*
HESIOD.—" The Shield of Hercules."

HE dragon is the most interesting and most frequently seen of all chimerical figures, and it is a remarkable fact that such a creature appears at an early period of the world's history to have been known in the East and in countries widely separated. Long anterior to the dawn of civilisation in the West of Europe, even in far-off China and Japan in the extreme East of Asia we find the dragon delineated in very much the same form in which it appears in our national heraldry.

The ancients conceived it as the embodiment of

malignant and destructive power, and with attributes
of the most terrible kind. Classic story makes us
acquainted with many dreadful monsters of the
dragon kind, to which reference will afterwards be
more particularly made.

It is often argued that the monsters of tradition
are but the personification of solar influences, storms,
the desert wind, the great deeps, rivers inundating
their banks, or other violent phenomena of nature,
and so, no doubt, they are, and have been; but the
strange fact remains that the same draconic form
with slight modifications constantly appears as the
type of the thing most dreaded, and instead of melt-
ing into an abstraction and dying out of view, it has
remained from age to age, in form, distinctly a
ferocious flying reptile, until in the opinion of many
the tradition has been justified by prosaic science.
It is surprising to find that the popular conception of
the dragon—founded on tradition, passed on through
hundreds of generations—not only retains its identity,
but bears a startling resemblance to the original
antediluvian saurians, whose fossil remains now come
to light through geological research, almost proving
the marvellous power of tradition and the veracity of
those who passed it on.

Mr. Moncure Conway ("Demonology, or Devil
Lore") says: "The opinion has steadily gained that
the conventional dragon is the traditional form of
some huge saurian. It has been suggested that
some of those extinct saurians may have been con-

temporaneous with the earliest men, and that traditions of conflicts with them, transmitted orally and
pictorially, have resulted in preserving their forms in
fable proximately."

"Among the geological specimens in the British
Museum," says Hugh Miller, "the visitor sees
shapes that more than rival in strangeness the great
dragons and griffins of mediæval legends; enormous
jaws, bristling with pointed teeth, gape horrid, in
stone, under staring eye-sockets a foot in diameter;
and necks that half equal in length the entire body of
a boa-constrictor. And here we see a winged dragon
that, armed with sharp teeth and strong claws, has
careered through the air on leathern wings like those
of a bat." We are also told in the sacred Scriptures
by Moses of "fiery serpents," and by Isaiah of "a
fiery flying serpent." Other monsters—dragons,
cockatrices, and some of whose form we have no
conception—are also mentioned. Euripides describes a dragon or snake breathing forth fire and
slaughter, and rowing its way with its wings. It is
evident that such a creature may at one time have
existed. Looking at the widespread belief in dragons,
there seems little doubt that the semi-myth of
to-day is the traditional successor of a really once-
existent animal, whose huge size, snake-like appearance, and possibly dangerous powers of offence made
him so terrible that the earlier races of mankind
adopted him unanimously as the most fearful embodiment of animal ferocity to be found.

One of the latest acquisitions in the Natural History Museum, South Kensington, is the skeleton of that enormous creature the long-limbed dinosaur (*Diplodicus Carnegii*), recently discovered in America, eighty-nine feet in length from the head to the tip of the tail, the huge bulky framework of the monster measuring eleven feet in height at the shoulder. The enormous length of its neck and tail, with relatively small head, would indicate it to be an amphibious inhabitant of the waters, feeding on the vegetation growing in its depths.

Mr. Moncure Conway, in his remarkable work, "Demonology, or Devil Lore," describes all intermediate stages between demon and devil under the head of dragon. This he believes to be the only fabulous form which accurately describes all the transitions. Throughout all the representations of the dragon one feature is common, and that is the idealised serpent. The dragon possesses all the properties of the demon along with that of harmfulness, but differs from the devil in not having the desire of doing evil. The dragon in mythology is the combination of every bad feature in nature, all of which is combined into one horrible whole. "The modern conventional dragon," says Mr. Conway, "is a terrible monster. His body is partially green, with memories of the sea and of slime, and partly brown or dark, with lingering shadows of storm-clouds. The lightning flames still in his red eyes, and flashes from his fire-breathing mouth.

The thunderbolt of Jove, the spear of Woden, are in the barbed point of his tail. His huge wings—bat-like and spiked—sum up all the mysteries of extinct harpies and vampires. Spine of crocodile is on his neck, tail of the serpent and all the jagged ridges of rocks and sharp thorns of jungles bristle round him, while the ice of glaciers and brassy glitter of sunstrokes are in his scales. He is ideal of all that is hard, destructive, perilous, loathsome, horrible in nature ; every detail of him has been seen through and vanquished by man, here or there ; but in selection and combination they rise again as principles, and conspire to form one great generalisation of the forms of pain, the sum of every creature's worst."

" THE EXTERNAL FORMS OF DRAGONS are greatly dependent on the nature of the country in which they originate. In the far north, where exist the legends of the swan and pigeon, maidens and vampires, exists the swan-shaped dragon. As demons of excessive heat principally existed in the south, so in the north the great enemy of man was excessive cold. In the northern countries is found also the serpent element, but as serpents are there frequently harmless, this feature does not enter much into their composition. The CUTTLEFISH is supposed to have helped in the formation of the HYDRA, which in its turn assisted in forming the dragon of the Apocalypse. Assyrian ideas also seem to have assisted in the pictorial impersonations of the hydra. This many-headed monster is a representation of a torrent, which being cut off in one direction breaks out in another. The conflicts of Hercules with the hydra are repeated in those of the Assyrian Bel with Trinant (the deep), and also in the contentions of St. Michael with the dragon. The old dragon myths left in Europe were frequently utilised by the Christians. Other saints besides St. Michael were invested with the feats of Hercules ; St. Margaret, St. Andrew, and many others are pictured as trampling dragons under their feet. The Egyptian dragon is based on the crocodile, and this form being received into Christian symbolism did greatly away with other pagan monsters. The hideousness of the crocodile and the alligator could easily be exaggerated so as to suit the most horrible contortions of the human imagination. Amongst the most terrible dragons is Typhon, the impersonation of all the terrors of nature. Son of Tartarus, father of the harpies and of the winds, he lives in the African deserts ; from thence fled in fear, to escape his terrible breath, all the gods and goddesses. He is coiled in the whirlwind, and his many heads are symbolical of the tempest, the scrive, the hurricane, and the tornado."

Under the head of The Colonial Dragon Mr. Conway has embodied all the horrors and difficulties with which the early colonists would be beset. Amongst these he places the Gorgon and the Chimera. The most widely spread of all is the last named, and from it is supposed that all Christian and British dragons

are descended. The Christian myth of St. GEORGE
AND THE DRAGON is but a variation of BELLEROPHON
AND THE CHIMERA, in which the last has given place
to the dragon and the pagan hero to St. George.

"In ancient families there are usually traditions of
some far-distant ancestor having slain a desperate
monster. It is always the colonial dragon that has

Japanese Dragon.

been borrowed by poets and romancers. THE DRA-
GON killed by Guy of Warwick is but another
variation of the chimera. There is again the SOCK-
BURN WORM, slain by Sir John Conyers for the devouring of the people of the neighbourhood; the well-
known tradition of the LAMBTON WORM is in reality
a modification of the ARYAN DRAGON OF THE STORM-
CLOUD; smaller than a man's hand he swells out to
prodigious dimensions."

A favourite subject for Chinese and Japanese
painting and sculpture is a dragon very much of the

E

same type, and a monstrous representation of a dragon in the form of a huge Saurian still forms the central object at Japanese festivals.

Among the Chinese the dragon is the representation of sovereignty, and is the imperial emblem borne upon banners, and otherwise displayed as the national ensign. To the people of that vast country it represents everything powerful and imposing ; and it plays an important part in many religious ceremonies and observances. Dr. S. Wells Williams, the eminent sinalogue, describes the fabulous monster of Chinese imagination in the following passage : " There are three dragons—the *lung* in the sky, the *li* in the sea, and the *kiau* in the marshes. The first is the only *authentic* species according to the Chinese ; it has the head of a camel, the horns of a deer, eyes of a rabbit, ears of a cow, neck of a snake, belly of a frog, scales of a carp, claws of a hawk, and palm of a tiger. On each side of the mouth are whiskers, and its beard contains a bright pearl ; the breath is sometimes changed into water and sometimes into fire, and its voice is like the jingling of copper pans. The dragon of the sea occasionally ascends to heaven in waterspouts, and is the ruler of all oceanic phenomena." The fishermen and sailors before venturing away from land or returning to port, burn joss-sticks and beat gongs to ward off the evil influences of the dragon, and it is worshipped in a variety of ways. According to a fable current in China, the Celestial Emperor Hoang-ti was carried up to heaven, along with seventy other persons, by a great dragon ; those who were only able to catch at his moustaches were shaken off and thrown on the ground. It is still the custom when an emperor dies to say that the dragon has ascended to heaven. An eclipse the simple

JAPANESE IMPERIAL DEVICE.
The Dragon, the Ho-Ho, or Phœnix, and the Chrysanthemum.

Celestials believe to be caused by a great dragon that seeks to devour the sun or moon. A great noise is made by firing guns, beating drums, and the rattling and jangling of pairs of discordant instruments to frighten the monster away. A frequent subject of their artists is the dreadful dragon sprawling through masses of curling clouds in the act of grasping at or swallowing the great luminary, a subject which no doubt bears a deeper meaning than we see, and one intimately connected with their mythology.

In some of their splendid festivals the worship of the dragon is celebrated with great excitement and furore. On the Canton river a boat of immense length formed like a dragon in many wondrous folds, rowed by fifty or more natives, with wild music and dancing, and accompanied by a crowd of junks ; the unfurling of sails and the streaming of flags from the masts, the beating of drums, the noise and smoke from the firing of guns, all exhibit the fondness of a people for the pleasures of a national holiday.

Dragon's Teeth.—Cadmus slew the dragon that guarded the well of Ares, and sowed some of the teeth, from which sprang up the armed men who all killed each other except five, who were the ancestors of the Thebans.   Those teeth which Cadmus did not sow, came to the possession of Ætes, King of Colchis ;   and one of the tasks he enjoined on Jason was to sow these teeth and slay the armed warriors that rose therefrom.   The frequent allusion to the classic term *dragon's teeth* refers to subjects of civil strife ; whatever rouses citizens to rise in arms.

The mythical dragon has left the lasting impress of his name in various ways in our language and literature, as in the art of nearly every country.

☊ *Dragon's Head* and ☋ *Dragon's Tail.*—In astronomy *Nodes* are the opposite points in which the orbit of a planet, or of a moon, crosses the ecliptic. The ascending node marked by the character (☊), termed the *Dragon's head*, is where the planet or moon ascends from the south to the north side of the ecliptic, and the descending node indicated by the character (℧) the *Dragon's tail* is where it passes from the north to the south side.

Draco, a constellation in the northern hemisphere, representing the monster that watched the golden apples in the garden of the Hespèrides, slain by Hercules, and set as a constellation in the heavens.

Draco volens, a meteor sometimes visible in marshy countries—*Ignus fatuus*, or will-o'-the-wisp.

Draco volens, or flying dragon, a curious class of saurian reptiles peculiar to the East Indies, having membranous attachments to their limbs, which give them the appearance of flying as they leap from tree to tree.

Dragon's blood, a vegetable balsam of a dark red colour brought from India, Africa, and South America. So called from its resemblance to dried and hardened masses of blood.

The Dragon in Christian Art

(The symbol of the Supreme Spirit of Evil, or the Evil One)

It was believed that in the gloomy land of the Cimmerians and the confines of Hades strange monsters were to be met ; and not only there, but in any part of the universe which was conceived to be

beyond the pale of human habitation these weird
creatures might be encountered. The same idea is
recognised in the Semitic belief, that uncanny beings
lurked in the outer deserts, where men did not
penetrate at all, or did so only at great danger. The
"place of dragons" is associated with "the shadow
of death" (Ps. xliv. 19). Dragons are also associated
with the waters of the deep (Ps. lxxiv. 13) and are
called upon to praise Jehovah (Ps. cxlviii. 7) ; and
Isaiah (xxxiv.), describing in vivid and picturesque
language the destruction and utter desolation which
shall come on Zion's enemies, prophesies that her
palaces and fortresses " shall be a habitation for
dragons."

The term dragon is applied by the translators of
the Scriptures to some monsters of which we have
no knowledge. The word is used by ecclesiastics
of the Middle Ages as the symbol of sin in general
and paganism in particular, though ofttimes heresy
is denoted. The metaphor is derived from Rev. xii. 9,
where Satan is termed the Great Dragon ; in Psalm
xci. 13, it is said "the saints shall trample the
dragon under their feet."

In the book of Job we recognise in Leviathan a
creature more like the extinct saurians of the old
world than any crocodile recorded in historic times ;
and this leviathan is treated as still existing in the
days of David. In Psalm lxxiv. 13, 14, Jehovah
is spoken of as having broken the heads of the
dragons in the waters ; in Isaiah li. 9, as having

wounded the dragon; and pæans are sung on the punishment of "Leviathan, that crooked serpent," and the slaying of "the dragon that is in the sea" (Is. xxvii. 1). Finally, in the Apocalyptic vision, "there appeared another wonder in heaven ; and behold a great red dragon, having seven heads, and ten horns, and seven crowns upon his heads, and his tail drew the third part of the stars of heaven, and did cast them to earth " (Rev. xii. 3, 4) ; " I saw an angel come down from heaven, having the key of the bottomless pit and a great chain in his hand, and he laid hold on the dragon, that old serpent, which is the Devil and Satan, and bound him " (Rev. xx. 1, 2).

As a Christian emblem the dragon may be taken to symbolise the supreme spirit of evil, a veritable devil whom it

The Dragon of the Apocalypse.
By Albert Dürer.

was the special mission of militant saints to slay, as it had been the glory of the heroes of the pagan mythology to conquer. "In pictures of sacred and legendary subjects," says a late writer, "the dragon usually formed an important feature.   The evil thing was invariably depicted writhing under the foot of the saint, or transfixed with his triumphant spear.   In like manner *the virtues* trampled tranquilly each on her complementary vice, embodied in the form of some impossible creature ; and if the rigid virtues were sometimes insipid, it must be allowed that the demons were usually grotesquely characteristic, and often delightful in colour."

The prostrate attitude usually signifies the triumph of Christianity over Paganism, as in pictures of St. George and St. Sylvester ; or over heresy and schism,

St. Michael and the Old Dragon.
Arms of the Royal Burgh of Dumfries.

as when it was adopted as the emblem of the Knights of the Order of the Dragon, in Hungary, which was instituted for the purpose of contending against the adherents of John Huss and Jerome of Prague.

The dragon in Christian Art is often very variously represented, sometimes as a serpent, at other times as a dragon or wyvern, or again in the symbolic figure partly human, under which form we find the " old serpent " (the Devil) often represented, as in the conflict of St. Michael the Archangel. The numerous legends of saints who have fought and overcome dragons prove the symbolic light in which the impersonation of evil was generally viewed.

St. Margaret is the patron saint of the borough of LYNN REGIS, and on the old corporation seal she is represented standing on a dragon and wounding it with a cross. The Latin inscription on the seal is " Sub Margaret teritur draco stat cruce læta." The modern shield of the town is now blazoned : *azure three conger's* (or

From ancient carving.

dragon's) *heads erased and erect, the jaws of each pierced with a cross crosslet fitchée or.* In paintings St. Margaret is represented as a young woman of great beauty bearing the martyr's palm and olive crown, or with the dragon chained and helpless at her feet as an attribute. Sometimes she is depicted coming from the dragon's mouth, for the legend says the monster swallowed her, but on her making the sign of the cross he was compelled to free her again. A legend states that Olybus, Governor of Antioch, captivated by the beauty of Margaret, wished to marry her ; as she rejected him with scorn he threw her into a dungeon, where the devil appeared to her in the form of a horrible dragon and endeavoured to frighten her from her path.   Margaret held up the cross and the dragon fled.   Other legends say he burst asunder.

St. George and the Dragon.

" In many a church his form is seen,
    With sword, and shield, and helmet sheen :
    Ye know him by his steed of pride,
    And by the dragon at his side."

CHR. SCHMID.

ST. GEORGE, the patron saint of England, in his legendary combat with the monster, is a subject which occurs frequently in English sculpture and painting, and enters largely into the language and literature of the nation.   St. George appears to have been selected as the patron saint of England not long after the Norman conquest.   We find the anniversary of his martyrdom (April 23) was ordered to be observed as a festival by the National Synod of Oxford in 1222 A.D.

The "Golden Legend," printed by Pynson in 1507 (fol. cxix.), thus refers to "Saynt George" : " This blyssed and holy martyr Saynt George is patrone of this reame of Englōd : and ye crye of mē of warre; and in ye worsyp of whome is founded ye noble order of a garter : and also ye noble college in ye castell of Wyndsore, by Kynges of Englond. In whyche college is ye herte of Saynt George: whyche Sygysmond ye Emperour of Alamayn brought : and gaf it for a grete and precyous relyque to kynge Harry the fifte. And also the said Sygysmond was broder of the sayd garter. And also there is a piece of his head ; which college is nobly endowed to thonour and worshippe almighty God and his blyssed Martyr Saynt George. Then late us praye vnto hym that he be specyel protectour and defendour of this royaume."

The emblems commonly given to St. George, martyr, and patron saint of England are : a dragon, a shield bearing a red cross on a white field, and a spear. He is usually represented on horseback in the act of spearing the monster which is vomiting fire ; or as standing with the slain dragon at his feet.

That St. George is a veritable character is beyond all reasonable doubt, and there seems no reason to deny that he was born in Armorica, and was beheaded in Diocletian's persecution by order of Datianus, April 23, 303. St. Jerome (331-420) mentions him in one of his martyrologies ; in the next century there were many churches erected to his honour. St. Gregory (540–604) has in his sacramentary a "Preface for St. George's Day" ; and the Venerable Bede (672–735) in his martyrology, says : " At last St. George truly finished his martyrdom by decapitation, although the gests of his passion are numbered among the apocryphal writings."

According to the old ballad given in Bishop Percy's " Reliques of Ancient Poetry," St. George was the son of Lord Albert of Coventry. His mother died in giving him birth, and the new-born babe was stolen away by the weird lady of the woods, who brought him up to deeds of arms. His body had three marks : a dragon on the breast, a garter round one of the legs, and a blood-red cross on the arm. When he grew to manhood he first fought against the Saracens, and then went to Sylene, a city of Libya, where was a stagnant lake infested by a huge dragon, whose poisonous breath " had many a city slain," and whose hide "no spear nor sword could pierce." Every day a virgin was sacrificed to it, and at length it came to the lot of Sabra, the king's daughter, to become its victim. Decked out in bridal array she went out to meet the dragon ; she was tied to the stake, and left to be devoured, when St. George appeared in full panoply and mounted on his charger. He vowed to take her cause in hand, and when the dragon came on the scene it was encountered by the hero, who wounded it, and binding it to the lady's girdle it was

led like a "meek beast" into the city. St. George
there attacked it, thrusting his lance into its mouth,
killed it on the spot, and a church dedicated to Our
Lady and St. George was built to commemorate the
event. After many adventures he carried off Sabra
to England, where they were wedded, and at Coventry
lived happily till their death.

In his history of the Order of the Garter Mr. Antis
warmly censures those who would doubt the traditionary history of that saint, and says " he who would
credit St. Ambrose will not detract from the honour
of our George, the soldier and martyr of Christ,
concerning the dragon and the deliverance of the
beautiful royal virgin, which is related in so many
pictures," adding that " he shall not contradict those
who make an allegory of it, so that they do not deny
the certainty of this history. . . . Suppose every
one George, who being clothed with the virtue of
baptism and armour of faith, keeps his earthly body
in subjection by the due exercise of religion and piety,
and by the armour of the Spirit overcomes, and by
the true spiritual art crushes and confounds the
serpent's poison, the snares of the old Dragon, and
his diabolical arts and stratagems."

The dragon slain by St. George is simply a
common allegory to express the triumph of the
Christian hero over evil, which St. John the
Evangelist beheld under the figure of a dragon.
Similarly St. Michael, St. Margaret, St. Sylvester
and St. Martha are all depicted as slaying dragons ;

the Saviour and the Virgin as treading them under
foot ; and St. John the Evangelist as charming a
winged dragon from a poisoned chalice given him to
drink.   Even John Bunyan avails himself of the
same figure, when he makes Christian encounter
Apollyon and prevail against him.

A learned Frenchman, M. Clermont Ganneau, in
a treatise lately published, traces the legend of St.
George and the dragon to a very remote antiquity.
In the Louvre at Paris he found an Egyptian bas-
relief, which he identified as the combat of Horus
against Set, or Typhon, in the well-known Egyptian
legend.   It represents a man on horseback in Roman
armour slaying a crocodile with a spear ; but for the
fact that the rider has a hawk's head, the group
might easily be mistaken for the traditional combat
of St. George and the dragon.   Extending his in-
vestigations, M. Ganneau has brought to light some
most startling proofs of the connection between the
eastern and western mythologies.   We have therefore, he considers, evidence as clear and convincing
as evidence from deduction can be, that the Egyptian
" Horus and Typhon " ; the Greek " Perseus and
Andromeda " ; the " Bel and Dragon " of the
Apocrypha ; the Archangel Michael of Christian
legend who also slays the old dragon, are all one
and the same story with that of our own St. George.
We pass over the intermediate steps by which he
reconciles the divergent names and qualities of the
personages identified, and also the ingenious argu-

ments as to the real meaning of the symbolism in the worship of DAGON THE FISH-GOD.

In all the old romances dealing with feats of chivalry and knight-errantry the dragon plays an essential if not a leading part ; and a romance without some dragon or monster was as rare as one without a valiant knight or a beautiful lady. But of all the malignant creatures dreaded of gods and men, the most hateful and wicked is that prime dragon personified by Spenser under the type of the " blatant beast," and which confronts his hero, the Red Cross Knight, at every turn : " a dreadful fiend, of gods and men ydrad," who has a thousand tongues, speaks things most shameful, most unrighteous, most untrue, and with his sting steeps them in poison.

As an example of the inception and development of a dragon legend from slender materials, the following is related in Figuer's " World before the Deluge " :

In the city of Klagenfurth, in Carinthia, is a fountain on which is sculptured a monstrous dragon with six feet, and a head armed with a stout horn. According to popular tradition this dragon lived in a cave, whence it issued from time to time to ravage the country. A bold and venturous knight at last kills the monster, paying with his life the forfeit of his rashness. The head of the pretended dragon is preserved in the Hotel de Ville, and this head has furnished the sculptor for a model of the dragon on the fountain. A learned professor of Vienna on a visit to the city recognised it at a glance as the cranium of the fossil rhinoceros. Its discovery in some cave had probably originated the fable of the knight and the dragon—and all similar legends are capable of some such explanation when we trace them back to their sources and reason the circumstances on which they are founded. The famous bird, the roc, which played so important a part in the myths of the people of Asia, is also believed to have originated in the discovery of some gigantic bones.

Chief among DRAGON-SLAYERS of Christian legend we find the following :

St. Philip the Apostle is said to have destroyed a huge dragon at Hierapolis, in Phrygia.

St. Michael, *St. George*, *St. Margaret*, *Pope Sylvester*, *St. Samson*, Archbishop of Dol ; *Donatus* (fourth century), *St. Clement* of Metz, all killed dragons—if we may trust old legends.

St. Keyne of Cornwall slew a dragon.

St. Florent killed a terrible dragon who haunted the Loire.

St. Cado, *St. Maudet* and *St. Paull* did similar feats in Brittany.

The town of WORMS (famous as the place at which the Diet of Worms was held before which the reformer Luther was summoned) owes its name to the " Lind-wurm " or dragon there conquered by the hero Siegfried as related in the " Nibelungen Lied." (*See* p. 100.)

Drachenfels, on the Rhine (Dragon Rocks), is so called from the same monster ; and at Arles and Rouen legends are preserved of victories gained by saints over the *Tarasque* and *Gargouille*, both local names for the dragon. St. Martha conquered the fabulous Tarasque of the city of Languedoc, which bears the name of " Tarascon." Gargouille (water-spout) was the great dragon that lived in the Seine, ravaged Rouen, and was slain by St. Romanus, Bishop of Rouen, in the seventh century. The latter name has come down to us in the term " gargoyle," applied to the monstrous heads which often decorate the waterspouts of old churches.

A strange relic of the ancient faith is perpetuated in the remains of early Celtic art in the curiously wrought interlaced monsters which form the chief ornament of ancient Irish crosses, and particularly in the borders and initials of illuminated manuscripts, whose spirals and interminable interlacements of the most complex character, often allied with equally strange colouring, form a style perfectly unique in itself, and unlike any other ; the elaborate knots terminating in draconic heads, and with wings and animal extremities in wonderfully ingenious patterns that seem almost beyond the limits of human ingenuity. In the kindred art of Scandinavia we find similar decoration founded on serpentine forms.

Another survival of the dragon myth exists in the name given to some of our fighting men on the introduction of firearms. A kind of blunderbus gave

F

to the troops who used it the name of " dragoniers,"
whence is derived the well-known term dragoons.
They used to be armed with *dragons—i.e.,* short
muskets—which spouted fire, like the fabulous beast
so named.   The head of a dragon was wrought on
the muzzles of these muskets.   We have all heard of
the Dragonades, a series of persecutions by Louis
XIV., which drove many thousands of Protestants
out of France—and out of the world.   Their object
was to root out " heresy."   A bishop, with certain ecclesiastics, was sent to see if the heretics
would recant ; if not they were left to the tender
mercies of the Dragonniers, who followed these
" ministers of peace and good will to men."   The
same game of conversion was practised by the Re-
formed Church upon the Presbyterians of Scotland,
with its accompaniment of " dragons let loose "—in
which Claverhouse took a leading part.

" In mediæval alchemy the dragon seems to have
been the emblem of Mercury ; hence the dragon
became one of the ' properties ' of the chemist and
apothecary, was painted upon his drug pots, hung up
as his sign, and some dusty stuffed crododile hanging
from the ceiling in the laboratory had to do service
for the monster, and inspire the vulgar with a profound awe of the mighty man who had conquered
the vicious reptile."*

When apothecaries' signs were not derived from
heraldry, they were used to typify certain chemical

* " History of Signboards."

actions. In an old German work on alchemy one of the plates represents a dragon eating his own tail; underneath are the words which, translated, signify : " This is a great wonder and very strange ; the dragon contains the greatest medicament," and much more of similar import.

The Dragon in the Royal Heraldry of Britain

> " *Advance our standards, set upon our foes,*
> *Our ancient word of courage fair Saint George*
> *Inspire us with the spleen of fiery dragons.*"
> > "Richard III.," Act v. sc. 3.
> " *Come not between the dragon and his wrath.*"
> > "King Lear," Act i. sc. 2.

THE dragon does not seem to have been a native emblem with the Romans, and when they adopted it it was only as a sort of subordinate emblem—the eagle still holding the first place. It seems to have been in consequence of their intercourse with other nations either of Pelasgic or Teutonic race. Amongst all the new races which overran Europe at the termination of the classical period the dragon seems to have occupied nearly the same place that it held in the earlier stages of Greek life. Among the Teutonic tribes which settled in England the dragon was from the first a principal emblem, and the custom of

carrying the dragon in procession with great jollity
on May eve to Burford is referred to by old histo-
rians. The custom is said by Brand also to have
prevailed in Germany, and was probably common in
other parts of England.

Nor was the dragon peculiar to the Teutonic
races. Amongst the Celts it was the symbol of
sovereignty, and as such was borne on the sovereign's
crest.   Mr. Tennyson's " Idylls " have made us
familiar with " the dragon of the great Pendragonship " blazing on Arthur's helmet as he rode forth
to his last battle, and " making all the night a stream
of fire."   The fiery dragon or drake and the flying
dragon of the air were national phenomena of which
we have frequent accounts in old books.

The Irish *drag* means " fire," and the Welsh
dreigiaw (silent flashes of lightning) " fiery meteors ";
hence Shakespeare says :

"Swift, swift, ye dragons of the night !—that dawning
  May bare the raven's eye."
                                   Cymbeline, ii. 2.

A principal source of the Dragon legends in these
countries is the Celtic use of the word *"dragon"*
for " a chief."   Hence Pen-dragon (*sumus rex*), a
sort of dictator in times of danger.   Those knights
who slew a chief in battle slew a dragon, and the
military title soon got confounded with the fabulous
monster.   The name or title *Pendragon* (dragon's
head) was among British kings and princes what

Bretwalda was among the Saxons ; and his authority or supremacy over the confederation was greater or less according to his valour, ability, and good fortune. Arthur succeeded his father Uther, and was raised to the pendragonship in the first quarter of the sixth century.

The dragon was a symbol among the heathen. One of the sons of Odin was thus invoked : "Child of the Dragon, Son of Conquest, arise ! grasp thy silver spear ; thy snowy steed prepare and haste thee to the strife of the shield ! Uprise thou Dragon of Onslaught ! " And again :

> " Wave high the dragon's flaming sign,
>   Roll wide the shout of glee ;
>   Ho ! conquest ope thy crimson gates
>   This day I give to thee."

"The Dragon of the Shield struck his sounding war-board with his ponderous spada. The fierce-browed children of Hilda gathered round at the signal."

Maglocue, a British king who was a great warrior and of a remarkable stature, whose exploits had rendered him terrible to his foes, as a surname was called "The Dragon of the Isle," perhaps from his seat in Anglesey.

Cuthred, King of Wessex, bore a dragon on his banner. A dragon was also the device of the British King Uther Pendragon, or Dragon's-head, father or that King Arthur of chivalric memory, who so bravely withstood the incursions of the Saxons. *Two dragons addorsed*—that is, back to back—are ascribed to Arthur, as well as several other devices.

Dragon's Hill, Berkshire, is where the legend says St. George killed the dragon. A bare place is shown on the hill where nothing will grow, and there the blood ran out. In Saxon annals we are told that Cedric, founder of the West Saxon kingdom, slew there Naud, the pendragon, with 5000 men. This Naud is called Natan-leod, a corruption of Naud-an-ludh ; Naud, the people's refuge.*

Dragon Standard. From the Bayeux Tapestry.

" It has sometimes been thought," says Miss Millington, " that the royal Saxon banner bore a dragon; certain it is, that on the Bayeux tapestry a dragon raised upon a pole is constantly represented near a figure, whilst the words ' Hic Harold ' prove to be intended for Harold ; yet Matthew of Westminster, in describing a battle fought in the time of Edward I., says that the place of the king was ' between the dragon and the standard,' which seems to imply that the standard or banner had some other device. The dragon was perhaps a kind of standard borne to indicate the presence of the king. Henry III. carried one at the Battle of Lewes, fought against Simon de Montfort in 1264 :

---

* Brewer's " Dictionary of Phrase and Fable."

> " 'Symoun com to the feld,
>   And put up his banere ;
> The king schewed forth his scheld,
>   His dragon full austere.'

It was not, however, at that time restricted to the King, for Simon himself in the same battle

> " 'Displaied his banere, lift up his dragoun.'

The English at the Battle of Crecy carried a 'burning dragon, made of red silk adorned and beaten with very broad and fair lilies of gold, and broidered about with gold and vermilion.' This banner," adds Miss Millington, " perhaps resembled that used by the Parthians and Dacians, which is described by Ammianus Marcellinus as ' a dragon, formed of purple stuff, resplendent with gold and precious stones fixed on a long pike, and so contrived that when held in a certain manner, with its mouth to the wind, the entire body became inflated, and stretched its sinuous length upon the air.' "

" The dragon," says Mr. Planché, " was the customary standard of the kings of England from the time of the Conquest. It was borne in the battle between Canute and Edmund Ironside ; it is figured in the Bayeux tapestry, and there are directions for making one in the reign of Henry III., but it never formed a portion of their armorial bearings, i.e., as a charge upon the shield of arms."

Henry VII., first of the Tudor line, assumed as one of his badges the red dragon of Cadwallader—

" Red dragon dreadful." Henry claimed an unin-
terrupted descent from the aboriginal princes of
Britain, Arthur and Uther, Caradoc, Halstan, Pendragon, &c. His grandfather, Owen Tudor, bore
a dragon as his device in proof of his descent from
Cadwallader, the last British prince and first King
of Wales (678 A.D.), the dragon being the ensign of
that monarch. At the Battle of Bosworth Field
Henry bore the dragon standard. After the battle
of Bosworth Field Henry went in state to St. Paul's,
where he offered three standards. On one was the
image of St. George, on the other a " red fierce
dragon beaten upon green and white sarsenet " (the
livery colours of the House of Tudor) ; on the
third was painted a dun cow upon yellow tartan,
—the dun cow, in token of his descent from Guy
Earl of Warwick, who had slain

" A monstrous wyld and cruelle beaste
Called ye dun cow of Dunsmore Heath."

The dun cow is still one of the badges of the
Guards. This monarch founded the office of *Rouge
dragon pursuivant* on the day before his coronation
(October 29, 1485). Henry VII., Henry VIII.,
Edward V., Mary and Elizabeth all carried the
dragon as a supporter to the royal arms, but varied
in position, and at times superseded by a greyhound.
(A greyhound argent, collared or, the collar charged
with a rose gules, was a Lancastrian badge.)
Henry VIII. used for supporters the *red dragon and*

white greyhound of his family ; *a red dragon* and *a lion gardant gold,* sometimes crowned ; at other times *a silver greyhound* and *a golden lion, an antelope, a white bull, a cock,* &c. On the union of Scotland and England under King James, the Scottish *unicorn* was substituted for the sinister supporter, while the *lion gardant,* first adopted by Henry VIII., appears to have permanently superseded the red dragon of Wales, the white greyhound, &c., as the other supporter of the royal arms, the dragon being relegated to be the special badge of the principality of Wales, which position it still retains. The present royal badges, as settled at the union, 1801, are :

A white rose within a red . England.
A thistle . . . . Scotland.
A harp or, stringed argent, and a trefoil or shamrock vert . . . . Ireland.
Upon a mount vert, a dragon passant, wings expanded and endorsed, gules . . Wales.

Richard III. as a badge had a black dragon. " *The bages that he beryth by the Earldom of Wolst* (*Ulster*) *ys a blacke dragon,*" derived through his mother from the De Burghs, Earls of Ulster.

Mallet, in his " Northern Antiquities," states " that the thick misshapen walls winding round a rude fortress at the summit of a rock were called by a name signifying dragon, and as women of distinction

were, during the ages of chivalry, commonly placed
in such castles for security, thence arose the romances
of princesses of great beauty being guarded by
dragons, and afterwards delivered by young heroes

who could not achieve
their rescue until they had
overcome their terrible
guardians." The common
heraldic signification of a
dragon is one who has
successfully overcome
such a fortress, or it denotes the protection af-
forded to the helpless by
him to whom it was
granted, and the terror

A Dragon passant.

inspired in his foes by his doughty or warlike bearing. It was a title of supreme power among the
early British.

The dragon has always been an honourable bearing in British armoury, in some instances to commemorate a triumph over a mighty foe, or merely
for the purpose of inspiring the enemy with terror.
This seems to have been especially the case with the
dragon standard—the "red dragon dreadful" of
Wales (*y Ddraig Coch*) described as :

> " A dragon grete and grimme
> Full of fyre and eke venymme."

The Crocodile as the Prototype of the Dragon

In the existing representatives of the antediluvian saurians, the crocodile and alligator, we see the prototypes of the dragons and hydras of poetic fancy. The crocodile is a well-known huge amphibious reptile, in general contour resembling a great lizard covered with large horny scales that cannot be easily pierced, except underneath, and reaching twenty-five to thirty feet in length. The crocodile was held sacred by the ancient Egyptians, the Nile was and is its best-known habitat ; it is also found in the rivers of the Indian seas. Though an awkward creature upon land, it darts with rapidity through the water after fish, which is its appropriate food, but it is dangerous also to dogs and other creatures, as well as to human beings entering the water or lingering incautiously on the bank.

It is the *Lacerta crocodilus* of Linnæus, from Greek κροκοδειλος (*krokodeilos*) a word of uncertain origin. The Alligator, the American crocodile, takes its name from the Spanish *El Legarto*, the lizard. The Latin form is *Lacertus* or *Lacerta*.

Miss Millington, in her " Heraldry in History, Poetry and Romance," says that both dragon and crocodile seem anciently to have been confounded under one name, and that Philip de Thaun, in his " Bestiarus," says that " crocodille signifie diable en ceste vie." Guillim, an old heraldic writer, says :

" The dragons are naturally so hot that they cannot
be cooled by drinking of waters, but still gape for the
air to refresh them, as appeareth in Jeremiah xiv. 6."

Young, author of "Night Thoughts," in a foot-
note appended to the magnificent description of the
leviathan (crocodile), in his paraphrase of part of the
book of Job says : " The crocodile, say the naturalists,
lying under water, and being there forced to hold its
breath, when it emerges, the breath long repressed is
hot, and bursts out so violently that it resembles fire
and smoke.   The horse suppresses not his breath by
any means so long, neither is he so fierce and animated," yet the most correct of poets ventures to
use the same metaphor regarding him :

" Collectumque premens volvit sub naribus ignem."

The Heraldic Dragon

THE mythical dragon is represented in heraldic art
with the huge body of the reptile saurian type covered
with impenetrable mail of plates and scales, a row of
formidable spines extending from his head to his tail,
which ends in a great and deadly sting ; his enormous
jaws, gaping and bristling with hideous fangs, belch
forth sparks and flame; his round luminous eyes
seem to shoot gleaming fire ; from his nose issues
a dreadful spike.   He is furnished with sharp-pointed
ears and a forked tongue, four sturdy legs terminating in eagle's feet strongly webbed, clawing and

clutching at his prey. Great leathern bat-like wings
armed with sharp hook's points, complete his equipment. The wings are always "endorsed," that is,
elevated and back to back.

The dragon of our modern books of heraldry is
a miserable impostor, a degenerate representative of
those "dragons of the prime, that tore each other in
their slime." It is curious to note in this the gradual
degradation from the magnificent saurian type of the
best period of heraldic art to a form not far removed
from that given to an ordinary four-legged creature
covered with plates and scales. His legs are longer
and weaker, his mighty caudal appendage, shrunk to

insignificant and useless
proportion, and most un-
like his ancient proto-
type the crocodile. This
error of our modern
heraldic artists displays
remarkable lack of pro-
per knowledge of this
mythical creature and
his attributes. Such a
splendid creation of the
fancy should not be
represented in such a
weak and meaningless
form by the hands of

Crest, a Dragon's Head erased collared
and chained.

twentieth-century artists. The ancient form is infinitely to be preferred as a work of symbolic art.

✠ Domine · dirige · nos ·

ARMS OF THE CITY OF LONDON.—Two dragons are the supporters of the arms of the City of London, the crest a dragon's sinister wing. They are thus blazoned : *Argent a cross gules, in the first quarter, a sword in pale point upwards of the last. Supporters, on either side a dragon with wings elevated and addorsed, argent, and charged on the wing with a cross gules.*

The crest is *a dragon's sinister wing charged with a similar cross.*

THE COUNTY OF CHESTER has for its supporters two dragons, each holding an ostrich feather.

Basingstoke, Linlithgow and Dumfries on the town seals have St. Michael overthrowing the dragon (*see* p. 72).

The dragon appears in various forms in the arms of many towns, and also in those of some peers.

One of the most extraordinary and elaborate coats of arms of modern times is that of Viscount Gough. The sinister supporter of the shield is a dragon (intended to represent the device upon a Chinese flag). *A dragon or, gorged with a mural crown sable, inscribed with the word " China," and chained gold.*

Examples vary considerably in the form of the dragon, some early examples represent it to have four legs, others with only two, when it is properly a wyvern. The pendent " George " in the Order of the Garter represents it

Sinister supporter of the arms of Viscount Gough.

with a body similar to a crocodile, winged and covered with plates and scales.

A similar device to that of the George noble of Henry VIII. was the St. George slaying the dragon by Pistrucci, a foreigner employed at the mint. This handsome reverse, says Mr. Noel Humphrey, " Coin Collector's Manual," is nearly a copy from a figure in a battle-piece on an antique gem in the Orleans collection, but several Greek coins might equally well have furnished the model. Old George III. sovereigns and five-shilling pieces have this most finely conceived and executed device on the reverse of the coins. It also appears upon some sovereigns of Queen Victoria. Prominence is naturally given to the figure of St. George, the dragon in consequence being diminished in its relative size.

The Hydra

" Seven great heads out of his body grew,
An iron breast, and back of scaly brass ;
And all imbrued in blood his eyes did shine as glass,
His tail was stretched out in wondrous length."

SPENSER, " Faerie Queen," Book i. c. vii.

THE hydra is represented in heraldry as a dragon with seven heads; it is not of frequent occurrence as a bearing in armory.

Hercules and the Lernean Hydra.
From Greek vase.

The terrible dragon, with one hundred heads, that guarded the golden apples of the Hesperides, slain by Hercules, was celebrated in classic mythology ; so was the Lernean hydra, a monster of the marshes that ravaged the country of Lerna in Argolis, destroying both men and beasts. The number of its heads varies with the poets, though

ancient gems usually represent it with seven or nine.
Hercules was sent to kill it as one of his twelve
labours.   After driving the monster from its lair with
arrows he attacked it with his sword, and in place

The Hydra.

of each head he struck off two sprang up.   Setting
fire to a neighbouring wood with the firebrands he
seared the throat of the Hydra until he at length
succeeded in slaying it.   The fable is usually referred
to in illustration of a difficulty which goes on in-
creasing as it is combated.   (*See* page 63.)

"Whereon this Hydra son of war is born
  Whose dangerous eyes may well be charmed asleep."
                    Henry IV. part ii. sc. 2.

G

The Lernean hydra, the watchful dragon of the garden of the Hesperides, the many-headed Naga or snake of the Hindu religion, are, say learned writers, only some of the many forms under which the relics of the ancient serpent-worship exhibited itself.

A hydra, wings endorsed vert, scaled or, is the crest of *Barret* of Avely, Essex. It is also borne by the names *Crespine* and *Downes*.

A Wyvern holding a fleur-de-lis.

The Wyvern

(Saxon, *Wivere*, a serpent) said to represent a flying serpent, an imaginary creature resembling the dragon, but having only two legs, which are like an eagle's, and a serpent-like tail, barbed, sometimes represented nowed after the manner of serpents. It is figured on one of the standards in the Bayeux tapestry (*see* Dragon, p. 86). It is erroneously termed a dragon by some writers, though perhaps they may both be classed together. Old heralds say of these imaginary monsters that they are emblems of pestilence, and are represented as strong and fierce animals covered with

A Wyvern, wings endorsed, tail nowed.

invulnerable mail, and fitly typify viciousness and envy. In armory they are properly applied to tyranny or the overthrow of a vicious enemy.

Occasionally a wyvern is borne with the tail nowed and without wings.

Lindworm.—It is not usual to say a wyvern "without wings" or "without legs," but *sans wings* or *sans legs*, as the

Wyvern from the Garter plate of Sir John Gray, 1436 A.D.

case may be.   A dragon or wyvern sans wings is termed a lindworm.   (*See* page 80.)

Argent, a wyvern, wings endorsed gules, are the arms of *Drake*, of Ashe, Devon (Bart.), 1600.

The town of Leicester has for crest a *wyvern, wings expanded, sans legs, strewed with wounds, gules.*

Argent on a bend sable, between two lions rampant of the last, a wyvern volant in bend of the field, langued gules, Ruddings.

Two wyverns, wings endorsed and emitting flames, are the supporters of Viscount *Arbuthnot.*

The arms of the King of Portugal are supported by *two wyverns erect on their tails or*, each

Wyvern, or Lindworm.
(German version.)

holding a banner, the crest is a *demi-wyvern* out of a ducal coronet.

Guivre.—The wyvern or serpent in the arms of the Visconti, Lords of Milan, *argent a guivre d'azure couronnée d'or, issante de gules* (GUIVRE is represented as a serpent or wingless dragon sans feet, with a child's

body issuing from its mouth), is said to commemorate
the victory of a lord of that house over a fiery dragon or
guivre which inhabited a cavern under the church of
St. Denis in that place. " It is hardly possible," says
Miss Millington, "not to think that the story of the
dragon as well as its adoption in the coat-of-arms

Wyvern, wings displayed.
(Early example.)

Wyvern, wings depressed.

bears allusion rather to the dragon of paganism,
expelled from the city, as it might seem, by the
church built upon the site of the cave, in which too,
by the rite of Holy Baptism, *children* especially
were delivered from the power of Satan. Indeed,
the innumerable legends of saints who have fought
and overcome dragons sufficiently prove the symbolic
light in which that creature was anciently viewed."
(*See* also Serpent Biscia, p. 117.)

The Chimera

AN imaginary fire-breathing monster of great swiftness and strength, invented by the ancient Greek poets. Though mentioned by heraldic authorities, it is not met with in British coat armour ; it is described as having the head, mane and legs of a lion, the body of a goat, and the tail of a dragon. From this creature the term " chimerical " is applied to all such figures as have no other existence but in the imagination. It is represented upon the coins of Sycion during the Achæan League. The origin of the story of the chimera is ascribed to a mountain in Lycia which had a volcano on its top and nourished lions ; the middle part afforded pasture for goats, and the bottom was infested with serpents ; according to Hesiod it had three heads, that of a lion, a goat, and a dragon. Bellerophon destroyed the monster by raising himself in the air on his winged steed Pegasus, and shooting it with his arrows.

Chimera, from a
Greek coin.

> " Amid the troops, and like the leading god,
> High o'er the rest in arms the graceful Turnus rode ;
> A triple pile of plumes his crest adorned,
> On which with belching flames chimera burned :
> The more the kindled combat rises higher,
> The more with fury burns the blazing fire."
>
> VIRGIL, *Æneid*, Book vii.

Phillip II. of Spain, after his marriage with Queen
Mary of England, assumed as a device, Bellerophon
fighting with the chimera, and the motto, " Hinc
vigilo," the monster being intended by him for a
type of England's heresies which he waited his time
to destroy.

The family of *Fada* of Verona have for arms :
Gules a winged chimera argent, the head and
breasts carnation (or proper), and the wings and
feet of an eagle. The illustration, however, has the
head and breasts of a woman, and eagle's wings and
feet, and makes it a different creature entirely, and
should more properly be blazoned *harpy*.

The Lion-Dragon

is compounded of the forepart of a lion conjoined
to the hinder part of a dragon.

*Or, a lion-dragon gules armed, langued and crowned
of the first*, is the *Bretigni* family.

*Party per chevron gules and or, three lion-dragons
ducally crowned and countercharged.—Easton.*

The Gorgon

REFERENCE has already been made to the gorgon
in a quotation from Milton. The name now denotes
anything unusually hideous. In classic story there
were three gorgons, with serpents on their heads

instead of hair. Medusa was the chief of the three, and the only one that was mortal. So hideous was her face that whoever set eyes on it was instantly turned to stone. She was slain by Perseus, and her head placed upon *the shield of Minerva* (termed the Ægis of Minerva). Homer, in the "Odyssey," Book xi. thus alludes to the dread creature :

> "Lest Gorgon rising from the infernal lakes
>   With horrors armed, and curls of hissing snakes,
>   Should fix me stiffened at the monstrous sight,
>   A stony image in eternal night."

And Shakespeare, in *Macbeth*, Act ii. sc. 3, uses the name to picture, in a word, the horrible discovery of the murdered Duncan :

> "Approach the chamber, and destroy your sight
>   With a new gorgon."

The Cockatrice

THIS chimerical creature was said to be produced from a cock's egg hatched by a serpent ; hence its name. It differs from the wyvern of heraldry only in having a head like that of a dunghill cock. "This monster is of that nature," says an old writer, "that its look or breath is said to be deadly poison"; and this, in addition to the ordinary weapons of offence, would constitute it rather a difficult creature to be interfered with.

The cockatrice is frequently referred to in the Scriptures as the type of something evil. "The weaned child shall put his hand on the cockatrice's den" (Isaiah xi. 8), meaning that the most noxious animal shall not hurt the most feeble of God's creatures.

Cockatrice.

And Jeremiah viii. 17: "For behold, I will send serpents, cockatrices, among you which will not be charmed, and they shall bite you, saith the Lord."

The cockatrice is a frequent emblem in heraldry, borne as a charge upon the shield and also as a supporter. To the mailed draconic form of the wyvern it had the hideous crested head with livid dangling wattles similar to the dunghill cock, its round glittering eyes dealing death; its barbed tongue and serpentine tail, with deadly sting, would no doubt render it a fearful object to behold, and terrific to its enemies. It is always borne in profile, the wings endorsed, or back to back, unless directed otherwise. The tail is frequently *nowed*, *i.e.*, knotted.

Sable, a cockatrice or, combed and wattled gules.—Bothe.

Sable, a cockatrice, displayed argent, crested, membered and jelloped gules.—Baggine.

Jelloped, jowlopped, terms used to describe the comb or crest, and gills or wattles, when of a different tincture from the body. *Beaked* and *membered,* in similar manner, have reference to the beak and legs.

Basilisk, or Amphysian Cockatrice

THE amphysian cockatrice or basilisk in heraldry exactly resembles the cockatrice, but having an additional head (like that of a dragon) at the end of its tail instead of a barb or sting.

> "With complicated monsters' head and tail
> Scorpion and Asp and Amphisbœna dire."
>
> MILTON.

Amphisbœna, or *Amphista,* is a creature sometimes referred to by old writers as having the dragon's body and wings, the head of a serpent, and the tail ending in a like head. Bossewelle, in "A rmorie of Honour," folio 63, enlarging upon this idea, describes "a prodigious serpente called Amphybene, for that he hath a double head, as though one mouth were too little to custe his venyme."

Earl Howe has for supporters *two cockatrices (amphysian), wings elevated, the tails nowed, and ending in a serpent's head or, combed, wattled and legged gules.*

Argent, a basilisk, wings endorsed, tail nowed, sable. —*Langley,* Rathorpe Hall, Yorks.

Basilisk, the king of serpents (Greek, *Basileus*, a king), so called from having on his head a mitre-shaped crest. Old writers give wonderful accounts of the death-dealing power of this strange creature. Pliny says, "all other serpents do flee from and are afraid of it," and tells of the deadly effect of his breath and glittering eye. The Duke of Alva, the scourge of the Netherlands (1566-1575), where he left the eternal memory of his cruelties, had for a device a basilisk drawing out serpents, with the motto :

Basilisk or Amphysian Cockatrice, tail nowed.

" Tu nomine tantum " ("Thou dost so much by thy name alone"), a fitting emblem for so great a monster !

In allusion to its power of "looking any one dead on whom it fixed its eyes," Dryden makes Clytus say to Alexander, "Nay, frown not so ; you cannot look me dead,"

> "like a boar
> Plunging his tusk in mastiff's gore,
> Or basilisk, when roused, whose breath,
> Teeth, sting and eyeballs all are death."
>
> KING, *Art of Love.*

King Henry, when he hears of the death of his

uncle Humphry, the good Duke of Gloucester, says
to Suffolk :

> "come basilisk
> And kill the innocent gazer with thy sight."
>
> 2 *King Henry VI.* Act iii. 2.

Beaumont and Fletcher also speak of " the basilisk's
death-dealing eye " in " The Woman Hater."

Its appearance was so dreadful, it was said, that if
a mirror was placed so that it could see itself, it
would instantly burst asunder with horror and fear.

In Christian Art it is the emblem of *deadly sin*
and *the spirit of evil.* St. Basil the Great uses it as
the type of a depraved woman.

The Mythical Serpent

"THE most remarkable remembrance," says Dean,
" of the power of the paradisaical serpent is displayed
in the position which he retains in Tartarus. A
cuno-draconictic cerberus guards the gates ; serpents
are coiled upon the chariot wheels of Proserpine ;
serpents pave the abyss of torment ; and even serpents constitute the caduceus of Mercury, the talis-
man which he holds in his hand when he conveys
the soul to Tartarus. The image of the serpent is
stamped upon every mythological fable connected
with the realms of Pluto. Is it not probable that
in the universal symbol of heathen idolatry we recognise the universal object of primitive worship, the
serpent of paradise ? "

" Speaking of the names of the snake tribe in the great languages," Ruskin says, "in Greek, OPHIS meant the seeing creature, especially one that sees all round it; and DRAKON, one that looks well into a thing or person. In Latin, ANGUIS, was the strangler; SERPENS, the winding creature; COLUBER, the coiling animal. In our own Saxon the SNAKE meant the crawling creature; and ADDER denoted the groveller."

The true serpents comprise the genera without a sternum or breastbone, in which there is no vestige of shoulder, but where the ribs surround a great part of the circumference of the trunk. To the venomous kind belong the rattlesnake, cobra de capello, spectacled or hooded snake, viper, &c. So the non-venomous, the boa constrictor, anaconda, python, black snake, common snake.

The minute viper, *V. Brashyura,* is celebrated for the intensity of its poison, and is truly one of the most terrible of its genus. The asp of Egypt, or Cleopatra's asp (*Coluber naja,* Lin.), was held in great veneration by the Egyptians; and it is this snake which the jugglers, by pressing on the nape of the neck with the finger, throw into a kind of catalepsy, which renders it stiff, or, as they term it, turns it into a rod.

All snakes, says the celebrated naturalist Waterton, take a motion from left to right or *vice versa*—but never up and down—the whole extent of the body being in contact with the ground, saving the head, which is somewhat elevated. This is equally observ-

able both on land and in water.   Thus, when we see
a snake represented in an up-and-down attitude, we
know at once that the artist is to blame.

Another misconception exploded by Waterton
is the common and accepted notion that a snake
can fascinate to their destruction and render powerless
by a dead set of its eye the creatures it makes its
prey.   Snakes have no such power.   The eyes, which
are very beautiful, do not move, and they have no
eyelids; they have been placed by nature under a
scale similar in composition to the scales of the body,
and when the snake casts it slough, this scale comes
away with it, and is replaced by a new one on a new
skin.

Noli me tangere—do not touch me with intent to
harm me—is, continues Waterton, a most suitable
motto for a snake, which towards man never acts on
the offensive (except perhaps only the larger species
which may be in waiting for a meal, when any creature, from a bull to a mouse, may be acceptable).   But
when roused into action by the fear of sudden danger,
'tis then that, in self-defence a snake will punish the
intruder by a prick (not a laceration) from the poison-
fang, fatal or not, according to its size and virulence.

A writer in the *Daily Telegraph* of July 23, 1883,
giving an account of the new reptile house in the
Zoological Gardens, Regent's Park, dwells upon the
surpassing beauty of a python that had just cast its
skin, " a very miracle of reptilian loveliness.   Watch
it breathing; it is as gentle as a child, and the

beautiful lamia head rests like a crowning jewel upon the softly heaving coils. Let danger threaten, however, and lightning is hardly quicker than the dart of those vengeful convolutions. The gleaming length rustles proudly into menace, and instead of the voluptuous lazy thing of a moment ago, the python, with all its terrors complete, erects itself defiantly, thrilling, so it seems, with eager passion in every scale, and measuring in the air, with threatening head, the circle within which is death. Once let those recurved fangs strike home, and there is no poison in them, all hope is gone to the victim. Coil after coil is rapidly thrown round the struggling object, and then with slow but relentless pressure life is throttled out of every limb. No wonder that the world has always held the serpent in awe, and that nations should have worshipped, and still worship, this emblem of destruction and death. It is fate itself, swift as disaster, deliberate as retribution, incomprehensible as destiny." It would be tedious to recapitulate the multitude of myths through which the " dire worm " has come to our times, dignified and made awful by the honours and fears of the past. A volume could hardly exhaust the snake-lore scattered up and down in the pages of history and fable.

" The python in the Zoological Gardens, however," adds the same writer, " though it may stand as the modern reality of the old-world fable of a gigantic snake that challenged the strength of the gods to overcome it, presents to us only one side of snake

nature. It possesses a surprising beauty and prodigious strength ; but it is not venomous. Probably
the more subtle and fearful apprehensions of men
originated really from the smaller and deadlier kinds,
and were then by superstition, poetry and heraldry
extended to the larger. The little basilisk, crowned
king of the vipers ; the horned ' cerastes dire,' a few
inches in length ; the tiny aspic, fatal as lightning
and as swift ; and the fabled cockatrice, that a man
might hold in his hand, first made the serpent legend
terrible; their venom was afterwards transferred, and
not unnatually, to the larger species. It was the small
minute worms, that carried in their fangs such rapid
and ruthless death, which first struck fear into the
minds of the ancients, and invested the snake with the
mysterious and horrid attributes whereunto antiquity
from China to Egypt hastened to pay honours."

Cadmus and his wife Harmonia were by Zeus
converted into serpents and removed to Elysium.
Æsculapius, son of Apollo, god of medicine,
assumed the form of a serpent when he appeared at
Rome during a pestilence ; therefore he is always
represented with his staff entwined with a serpent,
symbol of healing. Similarly represented was
Hippocrates, a famous physician of Cos; who
delivered Athens from a dreadful pestilence, in the
beginning of the Peloponnesian War, and was
publicly rewarded with a golden crown, and the
privileges of a citizen. Therefore it is that the
goddess of health bears in her hand a serpent.

The caduceus of Mercury was a rod adorned with wings, having a male and female serpent twisted about it, each kissing the other. With this in his hands, it was said, the herald of the Gods could give sleep to whomsoever he chose ; wherefore Milton, in " Paradise Lost," styles it " his opiate rod."

> " With his caduceus Hermes led
> From the dark regions of the imprisoned dead ;
> Or drove in silent shoals the lingering train
> To night's dull shore and Pluto's dreary reign."
> DARWIN, *Loves of the Plants,* ii. 291.

Jupiter Ammon appeared to Olympias in the form of a serpent, and became the father of Alexander the Great :

> "When glides a silver serpent, treacherous guest !
> And fair Olympia folds him to her breast."
> DARWIN, *Economy of Vegetation,* i. 2.

Jupiter Capitolinus in a similar form became the father of Scipio Africanus.

In the temple of Athena at Athens, a serpent was kept in a cage and called " The Guardian Spirit of the Temple." This serpent was supposed to be animated by the soul of Ericthonius. It was thus employed by the Greeks and Romans to symbolise a guardian spirit, and not unfrequently the figure of a serpent was depicted on their altars.

Upon the shields of Greek warriors, on ancient vases, &c., the serpent is often to be seen blazoned.

The serpent monster Python, produced from the mud left on the earth after the deluge of Deucalion,

lived in the caves of Mount Parnassus, but was slain by Apollo, who founded the Pythian games in commemoration of his victory. This and many similar solar myths are merely classic panegyrics on the conquering power exercised by the genial warmth of spring over the dark gloom of winter.

Greek Shield, from painted vase in the British Museum.

The serpent in Christian Art figures in Paradise as the tempter of Eve under that form, and is generally placed under the feet of the Virgin, in allusion to the promise made to Eve after the Fall : " The seed of the woman shall bruise the serpent's head." The heart of the serpent being close to the head, renders a severe " bruise " there fatal. The serpent bruised the " heel " of man—*i.e.*, being a cause of stumbling, it hurt the foot which tripped against it (Gen. iii. 15).

The brazen serpent erected by Moses in the wilderness, which gave newness of life to those plague-stricken Israelites who were bitten by the fiery dragons and raised their eyes to this symbol (Numb. xxi. 8), as an emblem of healing, is represented in Christian art as coiled up on a tau cross, a symbol of

which our Saviour did not disdain in some degree to

admit the propriety when he compared himself to
the healing serpent in the wilderness.

The serpent is placed under the feet of
St. Cecilia, St. Euphemia, and many other saints,
either because they trampled on Satan, or because
they miraculously cleared some country of such
reptiles. St. Patrick, the patron saint of Ireland, is
always represented habited as a bishop, his foot upon
a viper, the head transfixed with the lower extremity
of his pastoral staff, from his having banished snakes
and all venomous reptiles from the soil of Ireland.
As the symbol of the evil principle, a diminutive
specimen of the dragon, guivre, or winged snake was
more frequently used, wriggling under foot.

The serpent is emblematical of THE FALL ; Satan
is called the great serpent (Rev. xii. 9) ; of WISDOM :
" Be ye therefore wise as serpents, and harmless
as doves " (Matt. x. 16) ; of SUBTLETY : " Now the
serpent was more subtil than any beast of the field "
(Gen. iii. 1) ; of ETERNITY : a serpent in a circle
with its tail in its mouth is the well understood
symbol of unending time.

The serpent figures largely in Byzantine Art as the
instrument of the Fall, and one type of the Redemption. The cross planted on the serpent is found
sculptured on Mount Athos ; and the cross surrounded by the so-called runic knot is only a
Scandinavian version of the original Byzantine image
—the crushed snake curling round the stem of the
avenging cross. The cross, with two scrolls at the

foot of it typifying the snake, is another of its
modifications, and a very common Byzantine ornament.   The ordinary northern crosses, so con-
spicuous for their interlaced ornaments and grotesque monsters, appear to be purely modifications
of this idea." *

Boniface, the Anglo-Saxon missionary, in his
letter to the Archbishop of Canterbury, inveighs
against the luxuries of dress, and declares against
those garments that are adorned with very broad
studs and images of worms, announcing the coming
of Antichrist.

In the wonderfully intricate interlacing of snake-
like and draconic forms of celtic art which appear
in the marvellously illuminated manuscripts executed in Ireland of the sixth and seventh centuries,
the great sculptured crosses, as well as in gold and
metal work, are seen unmistakable traces of the
traditional ideas relating to the early serpent-
worship.

"The serpent," says Mr. Planché, "the most
terrible of all reptiles, is of rare occurrence in English
heraldry.   Under its Italian name of *Bisse* it occurs
in the Roll of Edward III.'s time, ' Monsire William
Mal*bis d'argent, a une chevron de gules, a trois testes
de bys rases gules* ' (*Anglicé*, argent, a chevron between
three serpents' heads erased gules)."

The well-known historic device, the *Biscia* or
serpent devouring a child, of the dukedom of Milan

* "Analysis of Ornament," by Ralph N. Wornum.

is of much interest. There are many stories as to the origin of this singular bearing. Some writers assign it to Otho Visconti, who led a body of Milanese in the train of Peter the Hermit, and at the crusades fought and killed in single combat the Saracen giant Volux, upon whose helmet was this device, which Otho afterwards assumed as his own. Such is the version adopted by Tasso, who enumerates Otho among the Christian warriors :

> "Otho fierce, whose valour won the shield
> That bears a child and serpent on the field."
> *Gerusalemme Liberata*, cant. i. st. 55.
> (Hoole's translation.)

From another legend we learn that when Count Boniface, Lord of Milan, went to the crusades, his child, born during his absence, was devoured in its cradle by a huge serpent which ravaged the country. On his return, Count Boniface went in search of the monster, and found it with a child in its mouth. He attacked and slew the creature, but at the cost of his own life. Hence it is said his posterity bore the serpent and child as their ensign. A third legend is referred to under Wyvern (which see).

Menestrier says that the first Lords of Milan were called after their castle in Angleria, in Latin *angus*, and that these are only the *armes parlantes* of their name.* Be this as it may, "*Lo Squamoso Biscion*"

* That is, *Visconti* is only a variation of *Biscia* equivalent to *Anguis*, Italianised to *Angleria*.

(the scaly snake) was adopted by all the Visconti lords, and by their successors of the House of Sforza.

> "Sforza e Viscontei colubri."
>
> *Orlando Furioso,* cant. xiii. 63.

And again in the same poem (cant. iii. 26. Hoole's translation) :

> " Hugo appears with him, his valiant son
>   Who plants his conquering snakes in Milan's town."

Dante also refers in " Purgatorio " to this celebrated device.

Arms of Whitby Abbey.

The " *three coiled snakes,*" which appear in the arms of Whitby Abbey, Yorkshire, really represent *fossil ammonites,* which are very plentiful in the rocky promontories of that part of the English coast, and on that account were no doubt adopted in the arms of the Abbey, and afterwards of the town of Whitby.

The arms are : *Azure three snakes coilea or encircled two and one, or.*

Popular legend, however, ascribes their origin to the transformation of a multitude of snakes into stone by *St. Hilda,* an ancient Saxon princess. The legend is referred to by Sir Walter Scott in "Marmion" :

> " How of a thousand snakes each one
> Was changed into a coil of stone
> While Holy Hilda prayed."

It is, however, more than likely that the arms suggested the legend of the miracle.

The ancient myth of the *deaf adder* seems to have been a favourite illustration of the futility of unwelcome counsel.

> " What, art thou, like the adder, waxen deaf ?
> Be poisonous too."
>
> 2 *King Henry VI.* Act ii. sc. 2.

> " Pleasure and revenge have ears more deaf than
>   adders
> To the voice of any true decision."
>
> *Troilus and Cressida*, Act ii. sc. 2.

> " He flies me now—nor more attends my pain
> Than the deaf adder heeds the charmer's strain."
>
> *Orlando Furioso*, cant. xxxii. 19.
> (Hoole's translation.)

A serpent or adder stopping his ears, by some writers termed " *an adder obturant his ear,*" from the Latin *obturo*, to shut or stop, is a very ancient idea. It is said that the asp or adder, to prevent his hearing unwelcome truths, puts one ear to the ground and stops the other with his tail, a device suggested by Psalm lviii. 4, 5 : " They are like the deaf adder that stoppeth her ear ; which will not hearken to the voice of charmers, charming never so wisely."

Alessandro d'Alessandri (+1523), a lawyer of Naples, of extensive learning, and a member of the Neapolitan Academy, took for device a serpent stopping its ears, and the motto, "Ut prudentia vivam" ("That I may live wisely"), implying that as the serpent by this means refuses to hear the voice of the charmer, so the wise man imitates the prudence of the reptile and refuses to listen to the words of malice and slander.

It is said that the *cerastes* hides in sand that it may bite the horse's foot and get the rider thrown. In allusion to this belief, Jacob says, "Dan shall be . . . an adder in the path, that his rider shall fall backward" (Gen. xlix. 17).

Asp.—According to Sir Gardiner Wilkinson, the ancient Egyptian kings wore the asp, the emblem of royalty, as an ornament on the forehead. It appears on the front of the double crown of Upper and Lower Egypt.

Many terms have been invented by the heralds to express the positions serpents may assume in arms. Berry's "Encyclopædia of Heraldry" illustrates over thirty positions, the terms of blazon of which it is impossible to comprehend, and hardly worth the inquiry. Few of these terms are, however, met with in English heraldry.

Two serpents erect in pale, their tails "nowed" (twisted or knotted) together, are figured in the arms of Caius College, Cambridge. In the words of the old grant, they are blazoned "*gold, semied with flowers gentil, a sengreen* (or houseleek) *in chief, over the heads of two whole serpents in pale, their tails knit together* (*all in proper colour*), *resting upon a square marble stone vert, between a book sable, garnish't gul, buckled, or.*"

Fruiterers' Company of London.—*On a mount in base vert, the tree of Paradise environed with the serpent between Adam and Eve, all proper.* Motto : *Arbor vitæ Christus, fructus perfidem gustamus.*

Nowed signifies tied or knotted, and is said of a serpent, wyvern, or other creature whose body or tail is twisted like a knot.

Annodated, another term for nowed ; bent in the form of the letter S, the serpents round the caduceus of Mercury may be said to be annodated.

Torqued, torgant, or *targant* (from the Latin *torqueo,* to wreathe), the bending and rebending, either in serpents, adders or fish, like the letter S.

Voluted, involved or *encircled, gliding,* and several terms used in blazon explain themselves, as *erect, erect wavy,* &c.

In blazoning, the terms *snake, serpent, adder,* appear to be used indiscriminately.

A Serpent, nowed, proper.
Crest of Cavendish.

A serpent nowed, proper, is the crest of Cavendish, Duke of Devonshire.

Gules, three snakes nowed in triangle argent (Ednowain Ap Bradwen, Merionethshire).

Or, three serpents erect wavy sable (Codlen, or Cudlen).

Remora is an old term in heraldry for a serpent entwining.

Serpents are also borne entwined round pillars and rods, &c., and around the necks of children, as in the arms of Vaughan or Vahan Wales : *Azure, three boys' heads affronté, couped at the shoulders proper, crined or, each enveloped or enwrapped about the neck with a snake vert.* Entwisted and entwined are sometimes used in the same sense.

Amphiptère, or flying Serpent.

The amphiptère is a winged serpent. *Azure, an amphiptère or, rising between two mountains argent,* are the arms of Camoens, the Portuguese poet.

As a symbol in heraldry the serpent does not usually have reference to the mythical creature, as in Early Christian Art, its natural qualities being more generally considered.

The Scorpion

THE reptile of this name, carrying a virulent and deadly sting in its tail, is generally borne erect. When it is borne with the head downwards, it is described as reversed. One branch of the family of Cole bears : *argent, a fesse between three scorpions erect sable;* and another branch of the same family, *argent a chevron gules between three scorpions reversed, sable.*

Scorpion.—Luigi di Gonzaga, styled Rodomonte for his great intrepidity and strength, was a favourite general of Emperor Charles V. in his army with Bourbon at the sack of Rome. When Charles made his public entry into Mantua, Rodomonte wore a blue surcoat made in squares. Upon one was embroidered a scorpion ; upon the other his motto, " *Qui vivens lædit morte meditur*" ("Who living wounds, in death is healed "). It being the property of the scorpion when killed and laid over the wound to cure the poison, so Rodomonte, if any one presumed to offend him, would clear himself of the injury by the death of his enemy.

Scorpion.

"If a man be stung with a scorpion, and drink the powder of them in wine, it is thought to be present remedie."*

* Pliny, Book xi. ch. 25, from an old translation.

Other Chimerical Creatures and Heraldic Beasts

Unicorn salient.*

The Unicorn

" *Yon lion placed two unicorns between*
  That rampant with a silver sword is seen
  Is for the king of Scotland's banner known."
                    Ariosto (Hoole's translation).
" *The lion and the unicorn fighting for the crown.*"
                    Old Nursery Rhyme.

HE unicorn is represented by heraldic usage as having the head and body of a horse, with the tail of a lion, and the limbs and hoofs of a stag; a twisted horn grows out from the centre of its forehead. It is rarely

* But for an oversight in the drawing, the unicorn should have been represented with the divided hoofs of a stag.

met with as a coat-of-arms. As a crest or supporter it is of more frequent occurrence. A unicorn's head is a favourite bearing, either *erased*, or *couped*, at the shoulder, and always represented in profile.

The unicorn was a famous device all over Europe, and symbolised the virtue of the mind and the strength of the body. It is well known as a supporter of the Royal Arms of England, a position it has occupied since the accession of James VI. of Scotland to the English throne as James I. *Two silver unicorns* were the supporters to the arms of that kingdom. On the legislative union with England, the *red dragon of Wales*, introduced by Henry VII., gave place to the unicorn as the sinister supporter.

Crest : A Unicorn's head, couped.

James III. of Scotland had it figured on coins which were thence called "unicorns." James V. first used it with the national arms as supporters. Although the silver unicorn came into England with James I., Queen Jane Seymour had already adopted it.

"*Unicorn*" was the pursuivant of Lord Lyon King-at-Arms, the Royal Scottish Herald.

As a supporter to the Royal arms it is thus blazoned : *A unicorn argent, armed, unguled, crined and gorged or, with a royal coronet* (*i.e.*, composed of crosses patée and fleurs-de-lis), *having a chain affixed thereto, and reflexed over his back of the last.* The term "*armed*" has reference to his horn, "*unguled*" to his hoofs, and "*crined*" to his flowing mane. "*Gorged*" implies that the coronet encircles his "gorge" or throat. The term "*or*" (that is, the metal gold or the tincture of it) being only mentioned after the several parts implies that they are all alike to be gold. "*Of the last*" means of the last colour mentioned.

In "The History of Caricature and Grotesque in Literature and Art," by Thomas Wright, M.A., F.S.A. (p. 8), appears a curious illustration from an Egyptian papyrus of the Roman period, in the British Museum. It represents a lion and a unicorn playing a game resembling draughts, perhaps the earliest instance of the two animals depicted in conjunction. As the author says: "The lion has evidently gained the victory and is fingering the money; his bold air of swaggering superiority as well as the look of surprise and disappointment of his vanquished opponent are by no means ill-pictured."

The animosity which existed between the lion and unicorn is referred to by Spenser, and is allegorical of the animosity which once existed between England and Scotland:

> "Like as a lyon whose imperiall powre
> A proud rebellious unicorne defyes."
>
> *Faerie Queen,* ii. 5.

I

Mediæval Conception of the Unicorn

THE mediæval conception of the unicorn as the
water-conner of the beasts was doubtless suggested
by that belief of earlier ages which made the unicorn
not merely symbolical of virtue and purity, but the
more immediate emblem of Christ as the horn of our
salvation (Psalms xcii. 10 and lxxxix. 17, 24), expressly
receiving its general fulfilment in him (St. Luke i. 69).
The horn, as an antidote to all poison, was also
believed to be emblematical of the conquering or
destruction of sin by the Messiah, and as such it
appears in the catacombs at Rome. The unicorn is
the companion of St. Justiana, as an emblem betokening in the beautiful legend her pure mind,
resisting all the Geraldine-like dreams sent by magic
art to haunt her, till she converted her tormentor
himself.

He is remarkable, say the old writers, for his
great strength, but more for his great and haughty
mind, as he would rather die than be brought into
subjection (Job xxxix. 10–12).

It was believed the only way to capture him was to
leave a beautiful young virgin in the place where he
resorted. When the animal perceived her, he would
come and lie quietly down beside her, resting his
head upon her lap, and fall asleep, when he would be
surprised by the hunters who lay in wait to destroy
him.

The unicorn is one of the most famous of all the chimerical monsters of antiquity. The Scriptures make repeated mention of such a creature, but of its shape we can form little conception. In Early Christian Art the unicorn symbolised the highest and purest virtue; not only was it one of the noblest bearings in the heraldry of the Middle Ages, but was

The Legend of the Unicorn.

viewed as the immediate emblem of our Blessed Lord. Philippe de Thaun says in his " Bestiarius " :

> " Monocéros est beste
> Une corne a en la tête
> Cette beste en verité nous signifie Dieu."

Whence comes the unicorn ? It is older than the days of Job. Among the hieroglyphics of Ancient Egypt this wonderful creature is depicted. Sometimes the body is that of an ass, sometimes that of a bull, sometimes that of a horse with the long twisted frontal horn for which he is noted. Is the myth derived from some mysterious single-horned antelope, as has been said, or is the one-horned rhinoceros the prototype of the legendary unicorn? As an emblem it figures on the obelisks of Nimroud and the catacombs of Rome. We read of this strange creature in Herodotus, and in Aristotle, who calls it the "wild ass"; Pliny calls it the "Indian ass," describing it as like a horse with a horn fixed in the front of his head. Cæsar counts it among the fauna of the Hyrcinian Forest. The earliest author who describes it is Ctesias (B.C. 400), who derives it from India. According to an Eastern legend the unicorn is found in Abyssinia. Lobo also describes it in his history of that country: there the animals are undisturbed by man, and live after their own laws. "Of the many ancient and famous men," says a modern writer, "who have written about the unicorn, no two seem to agree except when they copy from one another."

"Some writers" (says Guillim, p. 175) "have made doubt whether there be any such beast as this or no. But the great esteem of his horn (in many places to be seen) may take away that needless scruple."

The Horn of the Unicorn

" The unicorn whose horn is worth a city."
DECKER, " Gull's Hornbook."

The horn of the unicorn was supposed to be the most powerful antidote against, as it was a sure test of, poisons. He was therefore invested by the other beasts of the forest with the office of " water-conner," none daring to taste of fountain or pool until he had stirred the water with his horn, to discover whether any dragon or serpent had deposited his venom therein, and render it innocuous. So complete was the faith in the efficacy of the wonder-working horn as a test of poisons, that fabulous store was set upon the possession of even a portion. In old inventories the " Essai " of Unicorn's horn is frequently mentioned.

1391. Un manche d'or d'un essai de licourne pour attoucher aux viandes de monsigneur le Dauphin.— " Comptes Royaux."

1408. Une pièce de licorne à pour faire essai, à ung bou. d'argent.—Inv. des ducs de Bourgogne.

1536. Une touche de licorne, garni d'or, pour faire essai. —Inv. de Charles Quint.

An Italian author who visited England in the reign of Henry VII., speaking of the wealth of the religious houses in this country, says : " And I have been informed that, amongst other things, many of these monasteries possess unicorns' horns of an extraordinary size." Hence such a horn was worthy to be placed among the royal jewels. At the head of an inventory taken in the first year of Queen Elizabeth and preserved in the Harleian Library (No. 5953) we read " Imprimis, a piece of unicorn's horn,"which, as probably the most important object, is named first. This was no doubt the piece seen by the German traveller Hentzner, at Windsor : " We were shown here, among other things, the horn of a unicorn of about eight spans and a half in length, valued at about £10,000." Peacham places " that horne of Windsor, of an unicorn very likely," amongst the sights worth seeing.

"One little cup of unicorn's horn" was also in possession of Queen Elizabeth, and was subsequently given by James I. to his Queen.

Alviano, a celebrated general of the Venetian Republic, when he took Viterbo, and dispersed the Gatesca faction, whom he called the poison of the city, caused to be embroidered upon his standard a unicorn at a fountain surrounded by snakes and toads and other reptiles, and stirring up the water with his horn before he drinks, with the motto or legend " Venene pello " (I expel poison). Although the unicorn has not been seen and described by any modern writer, its horn has been occasionally found, sometimes preserved in museums, but alas ! the cherished horn, whenever it is examined, turns out to be a narwhal's tooth. To this, Wood's "Natural History " makes special reference : "In former days, an entire tusk of a narwhal was considered to possess an inestimable value, for it was looked upon as the weapon of the veritable unicorn reft from his forehead in despite of his supernatural strength and intellect. Setting aside the rarity of the thing, it derived a practical value from its presumed capability of disarming all poisons of their terrors, and of changing the deadliest draught into a wholesome beverage."

This antidotal potency was thought to be of vital service to the unicorn, whose residence was in the desert among all kinds of loathsome beasts and poisonous reptiles, whose touch was death and whose look was contamination. The springs and pools at which such monsters quenched their thirst were saturated with poison by their contact, and would pour a fiery death through the veins of any animal that partook of them. But the unicorn, by dropping the tip of his horn into the pool, neutralised the venom and rendered the deadly waters harmless. This admirable quality of the unicorn's horn was a great recommendation in days when the poisoned chalice crept too frequently upon the festive board, and a king could receive no worthier present than a goblet formed from such valuable material.

Even a few shavings of the unicorn's horn were purchased at high prices, and the ready sale for such antidotes led to considerable adulteration—a fact which is piteously recorded by an old writer, who tells us that " some wicked persons do make a mingle-mangle thereof, as I saw among the Venetians, being, as I here say, compounded with lime and sope, or peradventure with earth or some stone (which things are apt to make bubbles arise), and afterwards sell it for the unicorn's horn." The same writer, however, supplies an easy test, whereby the genuine substance may be distingushed from the imposition. "For experience of the unicorn's horn to know whether it be right or not ; put silk upon a burning coal, and upon the silk the aforesaid horn, and if so be that it be true, the silk will not be a whit consumed."

EXAMPLES.—*Argent, a unicorn rampant (sometimes sejant sable armed and unguled or*), is borne by *Harling,* Suffolk.

Another of the name bears the unicorn *courant in chief* with additional charges upon the shield.

Azure, a unicorn couchant, argent between twelve cross crosslets, or.—Doon.

Argent a chevron engrailed gules between three unicorns' heads, erased azure.—Horne.

Religious emblems were in great favour with the early printers ; some of them for this reason adopted the unicorn as their sign. Thus John Harrison lived at the Unicorn and Bible in Paternoster Row, 1603.

Again, *the reputed power of the horn* caused the animal to be taken as a supporter for the Apothecaries' arms, and as a constant signboard by chemists.

The great value set upon unicorn's horn caused the Goldsmiths of London to adopt this animal as their sign.

Pegasus or Pegasos.

The Pegasus

" The cheval volant—the pegasus—
He bounds from the earth ; he treads the air."

A POETIC creation of the ancients, a winged horse
captured by Bellerophon, the great hero of Corinthian
legend. In this he was assisted by the goddess
Minerva, who also taught him how to tame and use
it. At Corinth there was a temple erected to
Aθηναχαλινίτις (Minerva the Bridler), in allusion to
that part of the myth which describes Minerva as

instructing Bellerophon in the mode of placing the bridle on the winged steed. The legend states that the hero caught this wonderful animal as it descended at the Acro-Corinthus to drink of the spring of Pirene. Mounted on his winged steed Pegasus,

Bellerophon engaged the dire Chimera, and succeeded in destroying the monster by rising in the air and shooting it with arrows.

Pegasus is the steed of the Muses, and classic story ascribes to it the origin of the Castalian fountain "Hippocrene," situated on Mount Helicon, part of Parnassus, a mountain range in Greece. When the Muses contended with the daughters of Pieros, "Helicon rose heavenward with delight"; but Pegasus gave it a kick, stopped its rise, and there gushed out of the mountain "the soul-inspiring waters of Hippocrene."

Coins of Corinth and
Syracuse.

The Standard of Corinth was a winged horse, in consequence of the tradition connecting the fountain called Pirene, near the city, with Pegasus, the fiery winged steed of Apollo and the Muses. The same device was the leading type upon the ancient coins of the city of Corinth. The Corinthians founded the colony of Syracuse, in Sicily, which city likewise adopted the

winged horse and the head of Athena upon its
coinage.

Pindar, who grandly relates the feat of the hero
Bellerophon, says that he incurred the enmity of the
gods by attempting to fly to heaven on his winged

Pegasus salient.

horse. Zeus sent a gadfly to sting the horse, who
thereupon cast its rider and flew of his own accord
to the stables of Zeus, whose thunder-chariot he has
ever since drawn.

The pegasus is of frequent occurrence in heraldry.
In its classic allusions it denotes fame, eloquence,
poetic study, contemplation.

Some modern heraldic writers, however, discarding its classic references, regard it merely in the matter-of-fact light as an emblem of swiftness. But it is impossible to disassociate the old and well-known ideas respecting the horse of Apollo and the Muses. In fancy the poet mounts his winged steed to bear his soaring spirit in its wayward flight through the realms of fancy.

As a type of the perfect horseman, Shakespeare pictures Prince Henry as able to—

> " Turn and wind a fiery pegasus
> And witch the world with noble horsemanship."
>
> 1 *King Henry IV.*, Act 4, sc. 1.

Elsewhere he takes up the later interpretation of the myth, which connects it with Perseus :

> " The strong-ribbed bark through liquid mountains cut
> Like Perseus' horse."
>
> *Troilus and Cressida*, Act i. sc. 3.

Cardinal Bembo, poet and historian, secretary to Pope Leo X., used as his impress a pegasus and a hand issuing from a cloud holding a wreath of laurel and palm, with the motto, "Si te fata vocant" (" If the fates call thee ").

Azure, a pegasus salient, the wings expanded argent, is borne as the arms of the Society of the Inner Temple, London.

A very early seal of the Knights Templars exhibits two knights riding upon one horse.

A recent writer remarks upon this strange device that "it is exceedingly probable that some rude and partially defaced representation of this device was mistaken by the lawyers of the reign of Queen Elizabeth for a pegasus. The fact that the Middle Temple adopted the device which appears upon the other seal of the ancient Knights strongly confirms this view."

One of the supporters of the arms of Oliver Cromwell is a horse having the wings and tail of a dragon.

Sagittary, Centaur, Sagittarius, Centaurus, Hippocentaur

> " . . . the dreadful sagittary
> Appals our numbers."
> > "Troilus and Cressida," Act v. sc. 5.
>
> " Feasts that Thessalian centaurs never knew."
> > THOMSON, " Autumn."

UNDER these names is blazoned a fabled monster of classic origin, half man, half horse, holding an arrow upon a bended bow. It is one of the twelve signs of the Zodiac, commonly called Sagittarius, otherwise Arcitenens, and marked by the hieroglyph ♐. In its signification in arms it may properly be applied to those who are eminent in the field.

The arms traditionally assigned to King Stephen

are thus described by Nicholas Upton : " *Scutum rubeum, in quo habuit trium leonum peditantium corpora, usque ad collum cum corporibus humanis superius, aa modum signi Sagittarii, de auro,*"   In this, as in some

The Sagittary—Centaur.

other early examples, it is represented as half man, half lion.

The arms of Stephen are sometimes represented with but one sagittary, and is said to have been assumed by him in consequence of his having commenced his reign under the sign of Sagittarius. Others say because he gained a battle by the aid of his archers on entering the kingdom.   Others, again,

say that the City of Blois used the ensign of a sagittary as an emblem of the chase ; and Stephen, son
of the Compte de Blois, assumed that ensign in
his contest with the Empress Maude or Matilda.
There is no contemporary authority, however, it
must be confessed, for any of these derivations.
A sagittary is seen upon the seal of William de
Mandeville (*temp.* Henry III.), but not as an heraldic
bearing.

The crest of Lambart, Earl of Cavan, is : *On a
mount vert, a centaur proper, drawing his bow gules,
arrow or.* It also appears as the crest of Askelom,
Bendlowes, Cromie, Cruell, Lambert, Petty, Petty-
Fitzmaurice.

The term *Centaur* is most probably derived from
the words κεντέω (to hunt, or to pursue) and ταῦρος
(a bull), the Thracians and Thessalians having been
celebrated from the earliest times for their skill and
daring in hunting wild bulls, which they pursued
mounted on the noble horses of those districts, which
were a celebrated breed even in the later times of the
Roman Empire. A centaur carrying a female
appears on a coin of Lete, which, according to Pliny
and Ptolemy, was situated on the confines of Mace-
donia, and the fables of the centaurs, &c., in that and
neighbouring districts abounding in a noble breed of
horses, arose no doubt from the feats performed by
those who first subjugated the horse to the will of
man, and who mounted on one of these beautiful
animals and guiding it at will, to approach or retreat

with surprising rapidity, gave rise in the minds of the vulgar to the idea that the man and the horse were one being.

Sir John de Mandeville in his travels (printed by Wynken de Worde, 1499), tells us that in Bacharie

"ben many Ipotanes that dwellen sometime in the water and sometime on the land ; and thei ben half men and half hors and thei eten men when thei may take him."

Ipotane, from Mandeville's travels.

We have in modern history a singular and interesting example of a similar superstition. When the natives of South America —where the horse was unknown—first saw their invaders, the Spaniards, mounted on these animals and in complete armour, they imagined that the cavalier and steed formed but one being of supernatural powers and endowments.

Such groups as those exhibited on the rude money of Lete and other places were doubtless the first steps toward the treatment of similar subjects by Phidias, the celebrated Greek sculptor, whose works illustrating the battle of the Lapithæ and the Centaurs adorned the metopes of the Parthenon at Athens, to which they also bear a striking affinity in the simplicity of their conception.

A curious example of the compounded human and

animal forms similar to the sagittary is represented
upon a necklace found in the Isle of Rhodes, and
now in the Musée Cluny, Paris. It is formed of a
series of thin gold plates whereon is represented in
relief the complete human figure conjoined to the
hinder part of a stag (or horse).   This is alternated

Compound figures, gold necklace, Musée Cluny, Paris.

with another compound figure, human and bird,
holding up two animals by the tails, both subjects,
each in their own way, suggestive of the fleet and
dexterous hunter.

In Homer's account the centaurs are obviously no
monsters, but an old Thessalian mountain tribe, of
great strength and savage ferocity. They are merely
said to have inhabited the mountain districts of
Thessaly, and to have been driven thence by the

K

Lapithæ into the higher mountains of Pindus. Their contest with the Lapithæ is generally conceived as a symbol of the struggle of Greek civilisation with the still existing barbarism of the Early Pelasgian period. This may be the reason why Greek art in its prime directed itself so especially to this subject.

Centaur, Greek sculpture.

The origin of this contest is referred to the marriage feast of Pirithous and Hippodamia, to which the principal centaurs were invited. The centaur Eurytion, heated with wine, attempted to carry off the bride. This gave rise to a struggle for supremacy which, after dreadful losses on both sides, ended in the complete defeat of the centaurs, who were driven out of the country. The custom of depicting the centaurs as half man, half horse arose in later times, and became a favourite subject of the Greek poets and artists.

Amongst the centaurs, Chiron, who was famous alike for his wisdom and his knowledge of medicine, deserves mention as the preceptor of many of the heroes of antiquity. Homer, who knew nothing of the equine shape of the centaurs, represents him as the most upright of the centaurs, makes him the friend of Achilles, whom he instructed in music, medicine and hunting. He was also the friend of Heracles, who, by an unlucky accident, wounded him with a poisoned arrow. The wound being incurable, he voluntarily chose to die in the place of Prometheus. Jupiter placed him among the stars, where he is called Sagittarius.

Bucentaur, from Greek Βοῦς (bous) an ox, and κένταυρος (kentauros) a centaur, was, in classic mythology, a monster of double shape, half man, half ox. The state barge of the Doge of Venice was so termed.

The *Minotaur* slain by Theseus had the body of a man and the head of a bull.

Griffin or Gryphon

THE griffin, gryfin, or gryphon, as it is variously termed by old writers, is best known as one of the chimerical monsters of heraldry—the mediæval representative of the ancient symbolic creature of Assyria and the East. It may be classed with the dragon, wyvern, phœnix, sphynx, "gorgons and hydras and chimeras dire," and other imaginary beings, that world of unreality grown up in the mind of man from the earliest times, the influence of whose terrors have exercised no little power in the progress of humanity.

A Griffin statant, wings endorsed.

This favourite bearing was very early adopted in English armory. So early indeed as 1167 A.D. we find it on a seal of Richard de Redvers, Earl of Exeter, attached to a charter at Newport, Isle of Wight. It also appears on a seal of Simon de Montacute (*temp.* Henry III. and Edward I.). It is one of the principal bearings in heraldry, either charged upon the shield, as the arms, or as the crest placed upon the helm, also as supporters to the shield

of arms of many noble and eminent families in this
country and the continent.

The *griffin*, " sacred to the sun," combines the
bodily attributes of the " cloud-cleaving eagle " and
the " king of beasts," that is, it has the head, neck,
wings, and talons of an eagle, conjoined to the hinder
parts of a lion.   It is usually represented with pro-

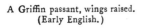

A Griffin passant, wings raised.   A Griffin segreant, wings displayed.
      (Early English.)   (German.)

jecting ears, indicating an acute sense of hearing, in
addition to its other supposed extraordinary qualities.

The griffin is rarely borne in other than two
positions, viz., *passant* and *segreant*.   The latter term
is peculiar to the griffin, and seems to refer to the
expanded wings.   When called *segreant* only, it
means the same as rampant applied to a lion.   As a
crest, it is not unfrequently borne *sejant*, *i.e.*, sitting.
Parts of the creature, as a *demi-griffin*, a *griffin's
head*, &c., are also of common use.

The arms of *Trafford*, Lancashire, are : *Argent a griffin segreant gules.*   Motto : *Gripe griffin hold fast.* The supporters of the arms of Viscount Halifax are two griffins.

Old heralds gravely relate of this creature that when he attains his full growth he will never be

Sleeping Griffin, by John Tenniel, from " Alice in Wonderland."
(By permission of Macmillan & Co., Limited, proprietors of the copyright.)

taken, hence he is a fit emblem of a valiant hero, who, rather than yield himself to his enemy, exposes himself to the worst of dangers.   As a general symbol in heraldry the griffin expresses strength and vigilance.

Sir Thomas Browne says it is emblematical of watchfulness, courage, perseverance and rapidity of execution.

The description of the griffin by the old traveller,

Sir John Mandeville, is a wonderful record of
credulity and belief in the marvellous; he states it to
be a native of " Bacharie, where ben many griffones,
more plentee than in any other countree. Sum men
seyn that they have the body upwards of an egle and
benethe as a lyonn, and truly they seyne soethe that
thei ben of that schapp. But one griffoun hath the
body more great and stronger than one hundred egles,
such as we have amonges us. For one griffoun there
will be flynge to his nest a great hors, or two oxen
yoked togidre, as thei gon to the plowghe. For he
hath his talouns so longe and so grete and large upon
his feet as though thei were hornes of grete oxen, or
of bugles (bulls), or of kygn, so that men maken
cuppes of hem to drynke of, and of hire (their) ribbes
and of the pennes of hire wenges men maken bowes
fulle stronge to schote with arrews and quarell."
Gerard Leigh, an old heraldic writer, discoursing of
the griffin, gives his reason for belief, he says, " I
thinke they are of a great hugeness, for I have *a
clawe* of one of their pawes, whiche should shewe
them to be as bigge as two lyons."

In the cathedral of Brunswick there is still preserved the horn of some kind of antelope, brought
from the Holy Land as " a griffin's claw," by Henry
the Lion. Three talons of the griffin were preserved
at Bayeux, and fastened on high festival days to the
altar, and there seems to be some curious legend concerning a cup formed of a gryphon's claw dedicated
to St. Cuthbert. A gryphon's egg was also con-

sidered a valuable curiosity, being used as a goblet in
old times when natural history was greatly misunderstood and grossly exaggerated.   As an example of
the absurd misstatements of the earlier writers and
naturalists who so delighted our wonder-loving forefathers, a writer in the " Museum of Animated

Griffin segreant, German version.

Nature" refers to a large species of vulture, the
Condor (*Sarcoramphus Gryphus*), which was painted
as rivalling the Rukh of Oriental fable.   He adds
that "such descriptions have given place to the
moderate details of sober-minded observers, and we
no longer look upon this creature as the winged
guardian of mountain mines within whose depths
were entombed 'gems and barbaric gold,' we no
longer imagine it the giant of the winged race,

dimming the light of the sun by its widespread pinions, and by the mighty rushing sound as it sweeps down from some lofty pinnacle or the upper regions of the sky deafening and stupefying the terror-stricken beholders."

As the stern avenger of human crimes, the dreaded Nemesis appears in Roman Art, as a young woman with wings, in a chariot drawn by griffins, with a whip or sword in her hand.*

Smith's "Classical Dictionary" gives the following: "Gryps or gryphus, a fabulous monster dwelling in the Rhiphæan mountains between the Hyperboreans and the one-eyed Arimaspians, and guarding the treasures of the north. The Arimaspians mounted on horseback attempted to steal the gold, and hence arose the hostility between the horse and the griffin. The body of the griffin was that of a lion, while the head, fore-feet and wings were those of an eagle. It is probable that the origin of the belief in griffins must be looked for in the East, where it seems they have been very ancient. They are also mentioned among the fabulous beasts which guarded the gold of India."

The Arimaspians were a one-eyed people of Scythia who adorned their hair with gold. They were constantly at war with the Gryphons who guarded the gold mines.

* "Mythology of Greece and Rome, with special reference to its Use in Art," from the German of O. Seemann.

" As when a gryphon, through the wilderness . . .
Pursues the Arimaspian, who by stealth
Had from his wakeful custody purloined
The guarded gold."

Paradise Lost, ii.

That the form of the griffin must have been a well
understood symbol is evident from the frequency
with which it is met in ancient art.   Dr. Schliemann,
in his explorations of the ancient city of Mycenæ,

Gold Flying Griffin, found by Dr. Schliemann at Mycenæ.

among other treasures found a gold-winged griffin,
about two inches in length, in one of the sepulchres
of the kings (Figure No. 272 in his book), which
in every particular as to shape is identical with the
heraldic griffin of to-day ; the same may be said of a
coin of Abdera, a city in Thrace, which bears the
device of a griffin. Abdera was a place of importance
when Xerxes invaded Greece B.C. 554.

Herodotus relates that the Teians, dreading the
encroachments of the Persians in Ionia, abandoned
their city and founded Abdera in Thrace. The coinage
of the latter place bears the same type (the griffin) as the

parent city, but with a slight difference in treatment. This consists in the form of the wings of the griffin, which are pointed on the coins of Abdera, while in those of Teos they are rounded. The griffin was sacred to Apollo, to whom an especial worship was

Colossal Griffins, Burmah.

devoted in most of the Ionian cities, but more particularly in Teos.*

In the *Illustrated London News* of October 21, 1876, is an engraving of two gigantic wingless griffons, and also a description by the traveller who visited that strange place. "At Thyetmo, 250 miles up the river Irrawaddy from Rangoon in British Burmah, are two colossal 'chin thay' or figures of

* W. N. Humphry's "Coin Collector's Manual."

sacred griffins, standing at the entrance to one of
the great pagodas dedicated to the worship of
Gautama Buddha; the outer terraces and steps of
these temples are frequently adorned with such
mythical monsters.   Near the ancient ruined city of
Paghan, which flourished a thousand years ago, the
bank of the river for a length of eight miles is lined
with the remains of this quaint architecture and
sculpture, covering a space of two miles in breadth
from the water's edge.   It is not known by what
nation of old times they were constructed, for
Burmese history is apocryphal or at least very
obscure."

The symbolic use of images of living creatures
was in the instance of the cherubim permitted under
the Mosaic dispensation, and on this will be found to
turn the distinction between the symbolic use and its
forbidden and dangerous use as a supposed means of
assisting devotion.   Mr. Henry Hayman in "Smith's
Dictionary," *s.v.*, "cherub," as quoted by Tyrwhit,
says : " On the whole it seems likely that the word
' cherub ' meant not only the composite creature-
form of which the man, lion, ox, and eagle were the
elements, but further, some peculiar and mystical
form which Ezekiel, being a priest, would know and
recognise as ' the face of a cherub,' κατ' εξοχήν, but
which was kept secret from all others. . . .   Such
were probably those on the ark, which when moved
was always covered, though those on the hangings
and panels might be of the popular device.   The

griffin of northern fable, watching the gold in the wilderness, has been compared with the cherub both as regards his composite form and his functions as guardian of a treasure. He goes on to point out the possible affinity between the Greek root γρυπ (γρυψ, gryps,' griffin), and the Hebrew and Arabic derivation of the word ' cherub,' which gives it the original meaning of ' carved image,' and says that though the exact form is uncertain, it must have borne a general resemblance to the composite religious figures found upon the monuments of Egypt, Assyria, Babylonia and Persia."

Mr. Ruskin,* describing the emblematical griffins on the front of the Duomo of Verona, points out that the Lombard carver was enabled to form so intense a conception, mainly by the fact that his griffin is a great and profoundly felt symbolism. Two wheels are under its eagle's wings, which connect it with the living creatures of the vision of Ezekiel, " where they went the wheels went by them, and whithersoever the spirit was to go, they went, and the wheels were lifted up over against them, for the spirit of the living creatures was in the wheels." The winged shape thus became at once one of the acknowledged symbols of the divine nature. Elsewhere, we think in the " Stones of Venice," the connection is pointed out between the Assyrian and Gothic personations.

Gian-Paolo Baglione (+ 1520), who usurped the

* " Modern Painters," vol. iii. ch. 8.

sovereignty of Perugia, bore a *silver griffin* on a red field with the motto, "*Unguibus et rostro atque alis armatus in hostem*" ("Armed against the enemy with talons and beak and wings "), which means of defence proved of no avail when he was seized by Pope Leo X., who, pretending to consult Baglione on affairs of importance, sent him a safe conduct to Rome, but when he arrived, he caused him to be tortured and beheaded, and afterwards took possession of his states. This gave occasion to his enemies to say, "This ugly bird has not used his wings as at other times, to flee from the snare which has been laid for him." *

In Dante's description of the triumph of the Church, in the "Purgatorio," we have the mediæval conception of this wondrous creature, the gryphon. "The mystic shape that joins two natures in one form "—as he is called by the noble Italian poet— draws the car to which he is harnessed, and

> "He above
> Stretched either wing uplifted 'tween the midst
>
> .   .   .   .   .
>
> And out of sight they rode. The members, far
> As he was bird, were golden ; white the rest,
> With vermeil interveined."

And when the eyes of Beatrice

> "stood
> Still, fix'd toward the gryphon, motionless.

---

* "Historical Devices, Badges, and War Cries," p. 10.

As the sun strikes a mirror, even thus
Within those orbs the twyfold being shone ;
For ever varying, in one figure now
    Reflected, now in other.   Reader ! muse
How wondrous in my sight it seem'd, to mark
A thing, albeit steadfast in itself,
Yet in its imaged semblance mutable."
                    Cary's Dante, *Purgatory*, c. xxix.

"Some commentators of Dante," says M. Dideron,*
" have supposed the griffin to be the emblem of
Christ, who, in fact, is one single person with two
natures ; of Christ in whom God and man are
combined.   But in this," says M. Dideron, " they
are mistaken.   There is, in the first place, a manifest
impropriety in describing the car as drawn by God as
a beast of burden."   "Commentators," it is added,
" have been misled by the two-fold nature of the
gryphon, but that difficulty is removed by recollect-
ing that the Pope resembles the eagle in his spiritual
character, and in his temporal authority the lion.
The Pope is one person, but of two natures and two
distinct forms.   Thus considered the allegory of
Dante becomes clear and intelligible."

The gryphon is very frequently seen sculptured in
Gothic churches, more especially in those of the
Lombard and early Norman style, and is evidently
intended to refer to the union of the divine and
human natures.

A curious example of this compound form of bird

* " Iconography of Christian Art."

and beast occurs on an Italian bronze medal of the fifteenth century, about $3\frac{1}{2}$ in. in diameter (No. 57.51 in the fine collection in South Kensington Museum). On one side it bears a portrait of Niccolo Picininus of

Carved panel, a Griffin segreant.

Perugia, a celebrated mercenary soldier—and on the reverse a griffin, the eagle's head, wings, and feet united to the Roman she-wolf, with Romulus and Remus suckling.   Dante's emblem of the Popedom is here apparently adapted to the peculiarly Roman national symbol—the nursing mother of nations and the Catholic religion.

The Male Griffin

THE griffin is sometimes borne sans wings and termed a *male griffin*, as in the supporters to the arms of the Marquis of Ormond, but spikes or rays proceed from various parts of its body ; sometimes it has two long straight horns.

Other Varieties of the Griffin

Two other varieties of the griffin family, the " *Hippogriff* " and the " *Simoorgh* " appear in the highly wrought imaginings of the poets, and may here be very briefly alluded to. They do not, however, appear in British Heraldy.

Male Griffin.

HIPPOGRYPH, or HIPPOGRIF, the winged horse whose father was a griffin and mother a filly (Greek, *hippos*, a horse, and *gryps*, a griffin)—a symbol of love.*

SIMOORGH, a sort of griffin or hippogryph, which took some of its breast feathers for Tahmura's helmet. This creature forms a very striking figure in the epic poems of Saadi and Ferdusi, the Persian poets.

---

* " Orlando Furioso," iv. 18, 19.

Milton also makes allusion to this mythical creature :

> " So saying he caught him up, and without wing
> Of hippogrif, bore through the air sublime
> Over the wilderness and o'er the plain."
>
> *Paradise Regained*, iv.

Opinicus statant.

The Opinicus, or Epimacus

This creature appears to be a variety of the griffin family. Authorities blazon it as having its body and four legs like those of a lion ; the head and neck and wings like an eagle, and the short tail of a camel, sometimes borne sans wings.

Such a monster with wings endorsed or, was the crest of the *Barber Surgeons of London*.

Two opinici vert, purfled or, beaked sable, wings gules, support the insignia of the *Plasterers' Company*.

Egyptian Sphynx.

The Sphynx

" That monster whom the Theban knight

Made kill herself for very heart's despite
That he had read her riddle, which no wight
Could ever loose, but suffered deadly doole."

SPENSER's " Faerie Queen," Bk. v. cxi.

ACCORDING to some heraldic writers, the sphynx should possess the head and bust of a woman, the paws of a lion, the body of a dog, and the tail of a dragon. In Lord Chancellor Bacon's book on " The Wisdom of the Ancients," there is an exposition of the meaning of the sphynx, which, says Dr. Woodward, is as curious as the creature itself.

It frequently figures in heraldry as a convenient hieroglyph to commemorate some service in Egypt. It is the crest of British families of *Asgill*, Baronets

Lambert, *Goatley*, &c., and appears in the arms of *Sir John Moore*, the hero of Corunna.

The strange combination of human and animal features in the figure known as the sphynx is of

Theban, or Greek Sphynx.

frequent occurrence in both Greek and Egyptian mythology and art. The Egyptian syhynx is supposed to represent the combination of physical power, or the kings, as incarnations of such attributes. They are also associated with the special forms and attributes of the great Egyptian deities Osiris and Ammon, Neph or Jupiter, and Phreh or Helios. That is, we have the *man-sphynx*, the *ram-sphynx*, and the *hawk-sphynx*, or the lion's body with the head of the man, the ram, or the hawk, according to the deity worshipped. The sphynx itself was probably a religious symbol of the Egyptians, which was transferred to Greece, and subsequently underwent a change of meaning. Among the Egyptians the sphynx seems to have been a symbol of Royal dignity betokening a combination of wisdom and strength. By the Greeks, however, it appears to have been regarded as the symbol of the burning pestilence-breeding heat of the summer sun. The form of the Theban sphynx was that of a lion, generally in a recumbent position, with the breast and upper part of a beautiful woman, and was in imitation of the original male sphynxes of Egypt. Greek Art was only acquainted with the sphynx in its female form, and also departed from the Egyptian type by adding wings to the lion's body.

"There is a great difference," says Sir Gardiner Wilkinson in his account of the sphynx,* " between the Greek and Egyptian sphynxes. The latter is human-headed, ram-headed, or hawk-headed, and is always male ; while the Greek is female, with the head of a woman, and always has wings, which the Egyptian never has."

In the Greek story the monster was sent by Hera (Juno) to devastate the land of Thebes. Seated on a rock close to the town, she put to every one that passed by the riddle, " What walks on four legs in the morning, on two legs at noon, and on three legs in the evening ? " Whoever was unable to solve the riddle was cast by the sphynx from the rock into a deep abyss. Œdipus succeeded in answer-

* " Manners and Customs of the Ancient Egyptians."

ing it, and thus delivered the country from the monster, who cast herself into the abyss.

The sphynx occurs upon a coin of Chios (B.C. 478-412). It is represented seated before an amphore, above which is a bunch of grapes. Chios was famed for its wine, and the sphynx was a symbol of Dionysius.*

The Emperor Augustus, on his seal, used the device of the sphynx—"maid's face, bird's wings, and lion's paws "—" implying," says Mrs. Bury Palliser (" Historical Devices," &c.), " that the secret intentions of a prince should not be divulged. When Augustus was in Asia, he authorised Agrippa and Mecænas, who administered affairs during his absence, to open and read the letters he addressed to the Senate before any one else ; and for this purpose he gave them a seal upon which was engraved a sphynx, the emblem of secrecy. The device gave occasion to ridicule, and to the saying that it was not surprising if the sphynx proposed riddles ; upon which Augustus discontinued it, and adopted one with Alexander the Great, to show that his ideas of dominion were not inferior to Alexander's. Subsequently Augustus used his own effigy, which practice was continued by his successors."

Maurice ("Oriental Trinities," p. 315) says the sphynx was the Egyptian symbol of profound theological mystery, and was therefore placed on either side of the *dromoi*, or paths leading to the temples

* W. Noel Humphry's " Coin Collector's Manual."

of the gods. "They are black," he says, "in allusion to the obscure nature of the deity and his attributes. The white head-dress may allude to the linen tiaras wrapped round the heads of the priests." The origin of the myth was not definitely known even to the ancients. Some early writers say it was symbolical of the overflowing of the Nile, which happened when the sun was in the signs of Leo and Virgo; and that it had its name from this circumstance. "For," they say, "the word sphynx in the Chaldæan language signifies overflowing." The fact of the Egyptian sphynx being always male does not, however, accord with this derivation.

A statue of the Theban sphynx found in Colchester, and now in the museum of that town, gives the Greek conception of that creature. It is carved in oolite, twenty-five inches high, evidently a relic of the Roman occupation of Britain. It represents the monster seated over the mangled remains of one of its victims. Llewellin Jewett, in the *Art Journal* 1871, p. 113, describes it as "combining the five-fold attributes of a virgin, a lion, a bird, a dog, and a serpent. The head, breast and arms are those of a beautiful virgin; the body and teats of a female dog; hinder parts, hind legs and fore paws are those of a lioness; the tail doubled in short folds is serpent, and the wings those of a bird."

The same writer says : "The sphynx appears on the reverses of some coins of Cunobeline (Cymbeline, of Shakespeare), struck in the city of Camalodunum (Colchester).

The gigantic statue of the sphynx half buried in the sand near the Great Pyramids, at Gizeh, is hewn and sculptured out of a spur of solid rock, to which masonry was added in places to complete the form. The actual age of the great sphynx is not known, but it is supposed to have been commenced under Cheops and finished by order of King Chefren, under whose reign also was probably built the second great pyramid. The able author of " Eothen " thus describes the appearance of the sphynx of Egypt, and the sentiments to which its contemplation gave rise in his mind : " And near the Pyramids, more numerous and more awful than all else in the land of Egypt, there rests the lonely sphynx. Comely the creature is, but the comeliness is not of this world. The once worshipped beast is a deformity and a monster to this generation, and yet you can see that these lips, so thick and heavy, were fashioned according to some ancient mould of beauty—some mould of beauty now forgotten—forgotten because that Greece drew forth Cytheræa from the flashing bosom of the Ægean, and in her image created new forms of beauty, and made it a law among men that the short and proudly wreathed lips should stand for the sign and main condition of loveliness through all generations to come ! Yet there still lives on the race of those who were beautiful in the fashion of the elder world ; and

Christian girls of Coptic blood will look on you with sad, curious gaze, and kiss your charitable hand with the big pouting lips of the very sphynx. Laugh and mock if you will at the worship of stone idols ; but mark ye this, ye breakers of images, that in one regard the stone idol bears awful semblance of deity—unchangefulness in the midst of change—the same seeming will and intent for ever inexorable ! Upon ancient dynasties of Ethiopian and Egyptian kings—upon Greek and Roman, upon Arab and Ottoman conquerors—upon Napoleon dreaming of an Eastern empire—upon battle and pestilence—upon the ceaseless misery of the Egyptian race—upon keen-eyed travellers—Herodotus yesterday and Warburton to-day—upon all, and more, this unworldly sphynx has watched, and watched like a Providence, with the same earnest eyes and the same sad, tranquil mien. And we shall die, and Islam shall wither away ; and the Englishman, straining far over to hold his loved India, will plant a firm foot on the banks of the Nile, and sit on the seats of the faithful ; and still that sleepless rock will lie watching and earnest the work of the new busy race with those same sad eyes and the same tranquil mien everlasting. You dare not mock at the sphynx." The conclusion of this rhapsody at the present time sounds almost like a half-fulfilled prophecy. ·

The sphynx is the special device of several British regiments which landed in Egypt, in the Bay of Aboukir, in the face of the French Army ; and borne as a memento of the battle of Alexandria, when General Sir Ralph Abercrombie fell in the moment of victory. It also appears upon the war medals of the English occupation of Egypt, resulting in the battle of Tel-el-Kebir, 1882, and subsequent victories. In heraldry the sphinx is usually couchant ; it is, however, borne in other positions, sometimes winged, and when so borne the wings are always endorsed, *i.e.*, back to back.

A sphynx passant, wings endorsed argent crined or, is the crest of Asgill (Bart. 1701).

A Sphynx passant guardant, wings endorsed.

The Phœnix.

The Phœnix Bird of the Sun

"Rara avis in terris."

An imaginary bird, described by ancient writers as
in form like an eagle, but more beautiful in its
plumage. Among the ancient classical writers it was
an emblem of those existing in paradise, enjoying
eternal youth and never-ending pleasure. Tacitus
decribes the phœnix as a singular bird, consecrated to
the sun, and distinguished by its rich appearance and
variegated colours. Herodotus naïvely says : "I

never saw one, indeed, but in a picture, but if he is like his picture his plumage is partly golden and partly red." Philippe de Thaun says : "The phœnix lives five hundred years and a little more, when it will become young again and leave its old age." It was said to be sometimes seen in Egypt, and only one was believed to exist at a time. When it is advanced in age and its time of change is at hand, it hides itself away somewhere in Arabia, and makes itself a nest of the rarest spices, which, by the heat of the sun or other secret agency, and the fanning of the sacred bird's own wings, soon rises into flames and consumes it. Out of its ashes rises another with new life and vigour to pursue the same never-ending life and re-birth.

Fum or *Fung* (the phœnix) is one of the four symbolical animals supposed to preside over the destinies of the Chinese Empire; the sacred *Ho-ho* or phœnix also figures with the dragon largely in Japanese mythology, and bears a striking analogy to the bird of classic fame. It is fabled to have a miraculous existence, and is sent on earth for the performance of extraordinary works in the manifestation of the Divinity and in the development of humanity and nature. It appears at different stages of the world's progress and in successive ages ; after the accomplishment of which it reascends to heaven to come down again at the commencement of a new era.

From the pagans the Early Christians adopted the

symbol, and with them its significance had reference to the resurrection and immortality. Like the pelican "in her piety," it was peculiarly an emblem of our Saviour in His resurrection. As the phœnix when old and wearied seeks the rays of the sun to consume its body, again to be revived in life and vigour, so the Christian, worn and exhausted by worldly labour and suffering, turns to the Son of Righteousness for regeneration and newness of life. Tertullian makes the phœnix an image of the resurrection.

In corroboration of this it must be borne in mind that Jesus Christ, who died A.D. 34, is termed *the phœnix* by monastic writers.

The Phœnix period or cycle is said to consist of 300 years. "The bird of wonder" is said to have appeared in Egypt five times :

    1. In the reign of Sesostris, B.C. 866.
    2. In the reign of Amasis, B.C. 566.
    3. In the reign of Ptolemy Philadelphus, B.C. 266.
    4. In the reign of Tiberius, 34 A.D.
    5. In the reign of Constantine, 334 A.D.

Tacitus in the "*Annales,*" vi. 28, mentions the first three of these appearances.

The *Phœnix-tree* is the palm. In Greek φοίνιξ (*phoinix*) means both phœnix and palm-tree. It is thus alluded to in Shakespeare :

> " Now will I believe . . . that in Arabia
> There is one tree, the phœnix throne—one phœnix
> At this hour reigneth there."
> *The Tempest*, Act iii. sc. 3.

Pliny * gives minute particulars concerning the natural history of this *rara avis in terris*. But the ancient fable is most fully given by Ovid and translated by Dryden. Ariosto, also, and many early writers refer to the wonderful creature with fullest faith in its reality. It is no wonder then, that it became a favourite emblem in an age when it was the fashion among persons of distinction to have an impress or device with its accompanying legend or motto. Many persons of historical importance employed the phœnix to express in metaphor the idea they wished to convey regarding themselves. Thus we find the phœnix in flames painted for the device of Jeanne d'Arc, in the Gallery of the Palais Royal, with the motto : " Invito funere vivat " (" Her death itself will make her live ").

Vittoria Colonna (+ 1547) the beautiful and accomplished wife of the Marquis of Pescara, used the device of a phœnix on her medal.

Mary Queen of Scots used the impress of her mother, Mary of Lorraine, a phœnix in flames, and the motto : " En ma fin est mon commencement." A phœnix in flames upon a castle was the badge of Queen Jane Seymour, the crest of the Seymours being a phœnix in flames issuing from a ducal coronet. Her son, Edward VI., added the motto, " Nascatur ut alter " (" That another may be born "), alluding to the nature of her death. She lies buried in St. George's Chapel, Windsor, with a Latin

* Book x. ch. 2.

epitaph by Bishop Godwin, which has been thus translated by his son Morgan :

> " Here a phœnix lieth, whose death
> To another phœnix gave birth.
> It is to be lamented much
> The world at once ne'er knew two such."

Queen Elizabeth placed a phœnix upon her medals and tokens with her favourite motto : "Semper eadem " ("Always the same "), and sometimes with the motto "Sola phœnix omnis mundi " ("The sole phœnix of the whole world"); and on the other side, " Et Angliæ gloria " (" And the glory of England"), with her portrait full-faced. By the poets of the time, Elizabeth was often compared to the phœnix. Sylvester, in his "Corona Dedicatoria," says :

> " As when the Arabian (only) bird doth burne
> Her aged bodie in sweet flames to death,
> Out of her cinders a new bird hath birth,
> On whom the beauties of the first return ;
> From spicy ashes of the sacred urne
> Of our dead phœnix (deare Elizabeth)
> A new true phœnix lively flourisheth."

And Shakespeare, in the prophecy which he puts into the mouth of Cranmer at the baptism of the Princess Elizabeth, her great and glorious reign is fore-shadowed, and finally :

> "... as when
> The bird of wonder dies, the maiden phœnix,
> Her ashes new create another heir,
> As great in admiration as herself."

Shakespeare elsewhere uses the simile to denote a phœnix among women—a phœnix, a paragon, unique, because alone of its kind :

> " If she be furnished with a mind so rare,
> She is alone the Arabian bird."
>
> *Cymbeline*, Act i. sc. 7.

Many other heraldic mottoes have been associated with this celebrated device. The following are from " Historic Devices, Badges," &c., by Mrs. Bury Palliser :

Eleanor, Queen of Francis I. of Austria : " Non est similis illi " (" There is none like her "). She afterwards changed her motto, either showing how much she was neglected, or to express her determination to remain single : " Unica semper avis " (" Always a solitary bird ").

Bona of Savoy : " Sola facta solum deum sequor."

Cardinal Trent : " Ut vivat " (" That it may live ").

Linacre : " Vivat post funera virtus " (" Virtue survives death ").

" De mi muerte ma vida " (" From my death my life ").

" De mort à vie " (" From death to life ").

" Et morte vitam protulit " (" And by death has prolonged his life ").

" Ex morte, immortalitas " ("Out of death, immortality").

" Murio y nacio " (" I die and am born ").

" Ne pereat " (" That it should not perish ").

" O mors, ero mors tua " ("O death, I shall be thy death").

" Se necat ut vivat " (" Slays himself that he may live ").

" Trouva sol nei tormenti il suo gioire ("It finds alone its joy in its suffering ").

" Vivre pour mourir, mourir pour vivre " ("Live to die, die to live ").

" Uror, morior, orior " ("I am burnt, I die, I arise ").

The phœnix in heraldry is never represented in other than in one position, *rising from flames*, that is, with expanded wings and enveloped in flames of fire in which it is being consumed. It is usually represented exactly as an eagle in shape, but may be of any of the heraldic tinctures.

The phœnix is of frequent use in heraldry, and borne by many families in the United Kingdom. A phœnix issuing from a ducal coronet is the crest of the Duke of Somerset.

Linacre, founder of the College of Physicians, and honorary physician to four sovereigns has on his tomb in Westminster Abbey the device of the phœnix, with the motto, " Vivat post funera virtus " ("Virtue survives death ").

From the association of this fabulous bird with alchemy, Paracelsus wrote concerning it, and several alchemists employed it to symbolise their vocation. It was adopted by the Apothecaries' Company as crest, and is a frequent sign over chemists' shops.

A phœnix in flames proper, gorged with a mural coronet, is the allusive crest of the Fenwicks ; the motto over the crest is the *cri de guerre*, " A Fenwick ! a Fenwick ! " They were a family noted in border warfare. " The house of Percy," says Mrs. Bury Palliser, " ever ranked the Fenwicks among the most valiant of its retainers, and in border warfare the

M

banner of the gorged phœnix in the burning flame always appeared with that of the silver crescent of the Percys."

The bird of paradise is interesting as having for a time been accepted as the veritable phœnix, a fact which has escaped Gibbon. That luxurious Emperor, Heliogabalus, having eaten, as he thought, of every known delicacy, bethought him one day of the fabled phœnix. What mattered it that only one bird existed at a time ; *that one*, the imperial gourmand must have, and was inconsolable that he had not thought of it before. The zeal of proconsuls was equal to the great occasion, and from all parts of the earth came strange and wondrous birds, each affirmed with confidence to be " the sacred solitary bird, that knows no second, knows no third." The canker-worm of doubt remains ! At last, one day there was brought to Rome from the far islands of the Eastern seas a bird, the like of which for the glory of its plumage had never been seen out of paradise, the veritable phœnix, " Bird of the Sun ! " The sight of the magnificent creature carried conviction with it. Heliogabalus ate in faith, and went to his fathers contented.

A Harpy, wings disclosed.

The Harpy

" *Of monsters all, most monstrous this ; no greater wrath*
  God sends 'mongst men ; it comes from depth of pitchy hell :
  And virgin's face, but womb like gulf unsatiate hath,
  Her hands are griping claws, her colour pale and fell."

VIRGIL.

  " *Thou art like the harpy,*
    Which to betray, doth wear an angel's face,
    Seize with an eagle's talons."

"Pericles Prince of Tyre," Act iv. sc. 4.

A POETICAL monstrosity of classical origin, described
as " winged creatures having the head and breasts of
a woman, and the body and limbs of a vulture ; very
fierce and loathsome, living in an atmosphere of filth
and stench, and contaminating anything which they

come near. Pale and emaciated, they were continually tormented with insatiable hunger." They are

The Harpy, Greek sculpture.

best known from the story of the Argonauts, where they appear as the tormentors of the blind king Phineus, whose table they robbed of its viands, which they either devoured or spoiled. They were regarded by the ancients as ministers of sudden death.

In Miss Millington's admirable book, "Heraldry in History, Poetry and Romance," it is stated that unlike the generality of such mythical beings, the harpies appear originally, as in Homer's "Odyssey," as persons instead of personations; while later authors for the most part reduced them to whirlwinds and whirlpools. Homer mentions but one harpy. Hesiod gives two, later writers three. The names indicate that these monsters were impersonations of whirlwinds and storms. The names were: *Ocypeta* (rapid), *Celeno* (blackness), *Aello* (storm).

> " I will . . . do any embassage . . . rather than
> Hold three woras' conference with this harpy."
> *Much Ado About Nothing*, Act ii. sc 1.

" Bravely the figure of this harpy hast thou
Performed, my Ariel ; a grace it had devouring."

Tempest, Act iii. sc. 3.

Azure, a harpy with her wings disclosed, her hair flotant, or, armed of the same. This coat existed in H u n t i n g d o n Church in Guillam's time.

The arms of the City of Nuremberg are : *azure, a harpy displayed armed, crined and crowned, or.* It occurs as the city device as early

A Harpy displayed and crowned.   German version.

as 1243.   In German heraldry it is termed *jungfraundler.*

A creature very similar to the harpy (a combination of several badges), was one of the favourite devices of Richard III., viz., a falcon with the head of a maiden holding the white rose of York.

Shield of Nüremberg.

The Heraldic Pelican

" Then sayd the pellycane
When my byrats be slayne
With my bloude I them reuyue (revive)
Scrypture doth record,
The same dyd our Lord,
And rose from deth to lyue."

SKELTON, " Armory of Birds."

THE character ascribed to the pelican is nearly as fabulous as that of the phœnix.   From a clumsy,

A Pelican in her piety, wings displayed.

gluttonous, piscivorous water-bird, it was by the growth of legends transformed into a mystic emblem of Christ, whom Dante terms " Nostro Pelicano."   St. Hieronymus gives the story of the pelican restoring its young ones destroyed by serpents as an illustration of the destruction of man by the old Serpent, and his salvation by the blood of Christ.

The Pelican in Christian Art is an emblem of Jesus Christ, by "whose blood we are healed."   It is also a symbol of charity.

The " Bestiarum " says that Physiologus tells us
that the pelican is very fond of its brood, but when
the young ones begin to grow they rebel against the
male bird and provoke his anger, so that he kills
them ; the mother returns to the nest in three days,

Heraldic Pelican in her piety.

sits on the dead birds, pours her blood over them,
and they feed on the blood.

Heralds usually represent this bird with wings
endorsed and neck embowed, wounding her breast
with her beak.   Very many early painters mistakenly
represented it similar to an eagle, and not as a natural
pelican, which has an enormous bag attached to the
lower mandible, and extending almost from the point
of the bill to the throat.   When in her nest feeding
her young with her blood, she is said to be IN HER
PIETY.

The Romans called filial love piety, hence Virgil's

hero is called the " pious Æneas," because he rescued his father from the flames of Troy.

The myth that pelicans feed their young with their

Crest, a Pelican vulning herself proper, wings endorsed.

blood arose from the following habit, on which the whole superstructure of fable has been erected : They have a large bag attached to their under-bill. When the parent bird is about to feed its brood, it macerates small fish in this bag or pouch ; then, pressing the bag against its breast, transfers the macerated food to the mouths of the young ones.

The pelican in her piety is not an uncommon symbol upon monumental brasses. That of William Prestwick, Dean of Hastings, in Warbleton Church, Sussex, has it with the explanatory motto : "Sic Xtus dilexit nos."

EXAMPLES.—*Gules, a pelican in her piety, or.*— *Chauntrell.*

Azure, three pelicans argent, vulning themselves proper.—Pelham, Somerset, &c.

A pelican's head erased, or otherwise detached from the body, must always be drawn in the same position and vulning itself. It should always be separated as low as the upper part of the breast.

It is said naturalists of old, observing that the pelican had a crimson stain on the tip of its beak, reported that it was accustomed to feed its young with the blood flowing from its breast, which it tore for the purpose. In this belief the Early Christians adopted the pelican to figure Christ, and set forth the redemption through His blood, which was willingly shed for us His children.

ALPHONSO THE WISE, King of Castile (+ 1252). A pelican in its piety. Motto : "Pro lege et grege."

WILLIAM OF NASSAU, founder of the Republic of the United Provinces, one of the noblest charac- ters of modern history. He bore on some of his

standards the pelican, and on others the motto :
" Pro lege, grege et rege."

POPE CLEMENT IX. One of his devices was the
pelican in its piety. Motto : " Aliis non sibi
clemens " ("Tender-hearted to
others, not himself ").

Other mottoes for the pelican :

" Ut vitam habeant " (" That
they may have life ").

" Immemor ipse sui " (" Un-
mindful herself of herself ").

" Mortuos vivificat " (" Makes
the dead live ").

" Nec sibi parcit " (" Nor spares
herself ").

The natural Pelican.

The Martlet

" *The guest of summer,*
The temple-haunting martlet."
" Macbeth."

THE MARTLET (*Merlette* or *Merlot*, French ;
Merula, Latin). The house-marten or
swallow is a favourite device in heraldry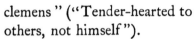
all over Europe, and has assumed a
somewhat unreal character from the
circumstance that it catches its food on
the wing and never appears to alight on the ground

as other birds do.   It builds its nest frequently
under the eaves of houses, from whence it can take
flight readily, rarely alighting, as it gains its food
while on the wing ; the length of its wings and the
shortness of its legs preventing it from rising should
it rest on the ground.

> " No jutty friese,
> Buttress, nor coign of vantage, but this bird
> Hath made his pendant bed, and procreant cradle."
>
> *Macbeth*, Act i. sc. 6.

It is depicted in armory with wings close, and in
profile, with thighs, but with no visible legs or feet.

The martlet is the appropriate " difference " or
mark of cadency for the fourth son.   Sylvanus
Morgan says : " It modernly used to signify, as that
bird seldom lights on land, so younger brothers
have little land to rest on but the wings of their own
endeavours, who, like the swallows, become the
travellers in their seasons."

The swallow (*hirondelle*) is the punning cognisance
for Arundell.   The seal of the town of Arundel
is a swallow, Baron Arundell of Wardour bears
six swallows for his arms.   The great Arundells
have as motto, " De Hirundine " (" Concerning the
swallow "), and " Nulli præda " (" A prey to none ").
A Latin poem of the twelfth century is thus rendered :

> " Swift as the swallow, whence his arms' device
> And his own arms are took, enraged he flies
> Thro' gazing troops, the wonder of the field,
> And strikes his lance in William's glittering shield."

"We find it in Glovers' roll," says Planché, "borne by Roger de Merley, clearly as 'armes parlantes,' although in a border." Roger de Merley : "*barée d'argent et de goulz à la bordure d'azur, et merlots d'or en le bordure*"; showing it was some difference of a family coat.

The Alerion

is a heraldic bird, represented as an eaglet displayed, but without beak or claws. Some writers confound it with the martlet, stating that the alerion

Alerion displayed.

Heraldic Eagle.

is the same bird with its wings displayed or extended. They are first found in the arms of Lorraine, which are blazoned *or, on a bend gules, three Alerions argent*, and are said to be assumed in commemoration of an extraordinary shot made by Godfrey de Boulogne, "who at one draught of his bow, shooting against David's Tower in Jerusalem, broched three feetless birds called Alerions, which the House of Lorraine, decending from his race, continued to this day." It is impossible, says Planché, who broached this wonderful story, but it is perfectly evident that the narrator was the party who drew the longbow, and not the noble Godfrey.

The letters of the word ALERION appear to be merely an anagram formed by the same letters LORAINE, and may account for the birds on the shield (probably eaglets) being called alerions.

The eagle displayed and the two-headed eagle are but extreme conventionalised representations of the natural bird.

The Liver (Cormorant)

LIVER, a fabulous bird, supposed to have given its name to Liverpool and commemorated in the arms of that city. It is traditionally described as a bird that frequented *the pool*, near which the town was afterwards founded. The arms granted in 1797 are thus blazoned : *Argent a cormorant, in the beak a branch of seaweed all proper*, and for crest, *on a wreath of the colours, a cormorant, the wings elevated, in the beak a branch of Laver proper*. It is more than probable that the bird on the arms suggested the name " Liver " being applied to it. The fiction naturally arose from the desire to find a derivation for the name of the town. It is, however, always depicted as a cormorant. On the shield the bird is always depicted with the wings *close*, and on the crest the wings are *elevated*.

An Heraldic Tigre passant.

The Heraldic Tigre or Tyger

" A savage tygress on her helmet lies ;
The famous badge Clorinda us'd to wear."
FAIRFAX'S " TASSO."

THE tigre or tyger of the old heralds still holds
its place in English armory, retaining the ancient
name to distinguish it from the natural tiger, to
which it bears but little resemblance except the
name. The early artists probably had no better
authority for the strange creature they depicted than
the wild tales of Eastern travel and their own lively
imaginations. The habit of drawing in a conventional manner may also have assisted in producing
such a monster. This type of wild and ruthless
ferocity, approaching the draconic in its power and
destructiveness, was to their minds fitly suggested

by exaggerations of those attributes of savageness
and bloodthirstiness with which it was supposed to
be endowed. Shakespeare makes King Henry V.,
when urging on his "noblest English" and "good
yeomen" to the assault at Harfleur, declare that

> " When the blast of war blows in our ears
> Then imitate the action of the tiger ;
> Stiffen the sinews, summon up the blood,
> Disguise fair Nature with hard-favoured rage."

"The tyger," says Bossewell, "is a beast wonderful in strength,
and most swift in
flight as it were an
arrow. For the
Persians call an
arrow tygris. He
is distinguished
with diverse
speckes ; and of
him the floode
Tygris tooke the
name. It is said
Bacchus used these
beastes in his
chariot, for their
marveilous swift-
ness in conveying of the same."

Supporter, an Heraldic Tigre, collared and lined.

The heraldic tigre, the invention of the early heralds,
is depicted as having the body similar to a wolf, but

more strong and massive ; powerful jaws armed with prominent canine tusks, and with a short curved horn or spike at the end of his nose. A row of knotted tufts of hair adorn the back of his neck as a mane ; tufts also on his breast and thighs, and with strong claws ; the tail of a lion completes his equipment. He is a most effective creature in a heraldic emblazonment, especially when " *armed* " and " *tufted* " of tinctures differing from his body.

The sinister supporter of the Marquess of Dufferin and Ava is *an heraldic tigre ermine, gorged with a tressure flory counter flory or.*

Gules a chevron argent, between three tigres, &c., *of the second.—Butler,* Calais.

Vert, a tigre passant or, maned and tufted argent.— Love, Norfolk (granted 1663).

Or, a tigre passant gules.—Lutwych, Lutwich, Salop.

Baron Harlech has for dexter supporter, and also for crest, *an heraldic tigre argent, maned and tufted sable.*

The tigre and mirror is an uncommon but very remarkable bearing. Amongst other remarkable ideas which our ancestors entertained respecting foreign animals, " some report that those who rob the tigre of her young use a policy to detaine their damme from following them by casting sundry looking-glasses in the way, whereat she useth to long to gaze, whether it be to beholde her owne beauty or because when she seeth her shape in the glasse she thinketh she seeth one of her young ones ; and so they escape the swiftness of her pursuit." *

" *Argent, a tigre passant regardant looking into a mirror lying fessways, the handle to the dexter all proper*," is said to have been the coat of Hadrian de Bardis (probably an Italian), Prebendary of Oxfordshire. These arms still remain, or were lately remaining, in a window of Thame Church. Only two other examples occur, viz. :

Tigre and Mirror.

" *Argent a tigre and mirror* (as before) *gules.*"—*Sibell*, Kent.

The Royal Tiger

NEXT to the lion in power is the tiger, an animal not possessed of the noble qualities of the lion, being fierce without provocation, and cruel without cause. The chief difference of the tiger from every other animal of the mottled kind is in the shape of the spots on the skin, which run in streaks or bands in the direction of the ribs. The leopard, panther and the ounce are all, in a certain degree, marked like this animal, except that the lines are broken by round

* Guillam's "Display of Heraldry." The same is also related in the Latin "Bestiarium," Harl. MSS. 4751 ; and by Albertus Magnus, Camerarius, &c.

spots, which cover the whole surface of the skin. The use of the *royal tiger* in modern coats of arms is frequent, and has reference to services in the East.

Outram, Bart., has for supporters : *two royal Bengal tigers guardant proper, gorged with a wreath of laurel vert, crowned with an Eastern crown.*

Note.—In a heraldic description (or blazon as it is termed) it is necessary for the sake of greater clearness, and to prevent confusion, to name the older mythical creature the "HERALDIC TIGRE," that it may not be confounded with its natural representative usually called the "ROYAL TIGER"

Leopard, or Panther, Felis Pardus, Lybbarde

"*Upon his shoulders a scheld of stele
With the lybbardes painted wele.*"
"The Metrical Romance of Richard
Cœur de Lyon."

"*Make the libbard stern
Leave roaring, when in rage he for revenge did yearn.*"
SPENSER, "Faerie Queen," Book i. canto vi.

A CURIOUS character, partly real and partly fictitious has been ascribed to the lybbard or leopard of heraldry. It was said to be the offspring of a lioness and a panther, the Northmen or Normans, according to some authorities, having adopted that beast of prey, noted for rashness, as typical of themselves, so charac-

terised by boldness and impetuosity. The standard
of Rollo, first Duke of Normandy, they say, bore a
leopard. A second lion or leopard was added to the
Norman shield when the county of Maine became
annexed to the Duchy of Normandy ; and the two
lions or leopards—for they
are indiscriminately so termed
—were thus borne, it is said,
upon the standard of William
the Conqueror, and by his
descendants. A third lion
was added by Henry II. on

A Leopard passant.

his marriage with Eleanor of Aquitain, a lion being
also the arms of that province.

It has been keenly contested whether the three
animals in the royal shield of England were lions
or leopards. The subject has been ably treated by
Mr. J. R. Planché in the " Pursuivant of Arms," and
also by Charles Boutell, M.A., in several of his works.
The case seems to stand thus :

In ancient coats the name is believed to be given
to the lion in certain attitudes. The French heralds
call a lion passant a *leopard*. Thus Bertrand du
Guesclin, the famous Breton, declared that men
" devoyent bien honorer la noble fleur-de-lis, qu'ils
ne faissaient le félon liépard," and Napoleon,
strongly to excite the valour of his soldiers, exclaimed,
" Let us drive these leopards (the English) into the
sea ! "

" *Lion Léoparde* " is the term used in French

heraldry for the lion when borne *passant guardant* as in the royal shield of England. When *rampant* they call it "léoparde lionné," as if in this attitude the leopard assumed the position and bold character of the lion. The attitude *passant guardant* thus denoted the peculiar stealthy tread and cat-like watchfulness of the leopard and panther.

The Emperor Frederick II. (1235) sent King Henry of England three leopards as a present in token of his armorial bearings.

It is a great argument in favour of the substitution of the lion for the leopard, Mr. Boutell thinks, that the latter should have almost disappeared from English heraldry, the face and head only retaining their place in modern coats.

A Leopard's Face, jessant-de-lis.

" *A leopard's head*" should show part of the neck, *couped* or *erased*, as the case may be; *guardant*, *affronté* or front face, is always to be understood of the leopard, and never in profile.

"*A leopard's face*" shows no part of the neck, and in conjunction with the term " *jessant-de-lis*," is used with respect to a leopard's face having a *fleur-de-lis* passing through it.

The insignia of the See of Hereford is : *gules three leopards' heads reversed jessant-de-lis, or.*

In heraldry the leopard represents those brave and

generous warriors who have performed some bold enterprise with force, courage, promptitude, and activity. Thus Shakespeare alludes to the character of the bold soldier

> " Full of strange oaths, and bearded like the pard,
> Jealous in honour, sudden and quick in quarrel,
> Seeking the bubble reputation
> Even in the cannon's mouth."

In Christian Art the leopard is employed to represent that beast spoken of in the Apocalypse, with seven heads and ten horns. Six of the heads are nimbed, but the seventh, being " wounded to death," has lost its power, and consequently has no nimbus.

Three leopards passant guardant or, pelletée, appear on the arms of the Marquis of Downshire. It is also the sinister supporter.

The supporters of the town of Aberdeen are leopards.

Sable three leopards rampant argent spottea sable are given as the arms of *Lynch.* It is, however, probable that the *lynx* was the animal originally blazoned as " arms parlantes " for the name.

Ermine on a cross patonce sable, a leopard's head, issuing out of a ducal coronet or, crest, *a demi-leopard erect, proper.—Dickens.*

A leopard's face, breaking with his mouth a sword, is the crest of *Disne.*

The supporters of the Earl of Northesk are *two leopards reguardant.*

The leopard or panther, says Dr. P. M. Duncan, F.R.S.,* was the only one of the greater feline animals, except the lion and tiger, which seems to have been known to the ancients. It is always represented as drawing the chariot of Bacchus, and the forlorn Ariadne is sculptured as riding on one of the spotted steeds of her divine lover. The panther was also constantly used in the barbarous sports of the amphitheatre, and, in common with the lion and tiger, has been both executioner and grave to many a bold-hearted martyr.

The leopard's skin was a favourite mantle in the olden times in Greece. In the "Iliad," Homer, speaking of Menelaus, says :

> " With a pard's spotted hide his shoulders broad
> He mantled o'er,"

and the leopard, or panther, is given in the " Odyssey " as one of the forms assumed by Proteus, " the Ancient of the Deep."

A curious ancient superstition about the leopard is embodied in its name. It was thought not to be actually the same animal as the panther or pard, but to be a mongrel or hybrid between the male pard and the lioness, hence it was called the lion-panther, or *leopardus*. This error, as Archbishop Trench tells us, " has lasted into modern times "; thus Fuller : " Leopards and mules are properly no creatures."

Some writers, says Boutell, describe the leopard as

* " Cassell's Natural History."

the issue of the pard and lioness, and they assign
the unproductiveness of such hybrids as a reason for
its frequent adoption in the arms of abbots and
abbesses. " Mulus et abbates sunt in honore pares."
The leopard and panther are now acknowledged
to be but slight varieties of the same species. In
Wood's " Natural History" some slight difference
is mentioned as to the number of spots. " The
panther is fawn-coloured above, white underneath,
with six or seven ranges of patches resembling rosettes
—that is to say, each composed of an assemblage
of five or six simple black spots. It very much resembles the leopard, which inhabits the same region
(but has ten rows of spots which are of smaller size),
It is the wildest of the feline tribe, always retaining
its fierce aspect and perpetual growl."

The Panther "Incensed"

" *The panther, knowing that his spotted hide*
Doth please all beasts, but that his looks them fray,
Within a bush his dreadful head doth hide
To let them gaze, while he on them doth prey."
SPENSER, Sonnet.

THIS beast, like the leopard, has been the object
of much mistaken or fictitious history. Pliny, who
is responsible for many of the errors in natural
history since his time, says of the panther : " It is
said that all four-footed beasts are wonderfully

delighted and enticed by the smell of panthers ; but their hideous looke and crabbed countenance which they bewray so soon as they show their heads skareth them as much again : therefore their manner is to

Panther incensed.

hide their heads, and when they have trained other beasts within their reach by their sweet savour, they fall upon them and worry them." * And again, Sir William Segar, Garter King-of-Arms, following the same credulous historian, says : " The panther is admired of all other beasts for the beauty of his skyn, being spotted with variable colours, and beloved of them for the sweetness of his breath that streameth forth of his nostrils and ears like smoke which our paynters mistaking, corruptly do make fire." †

It is, however, more probable that the creature was represented emitting flame and smoke to denote and give characteristic expression to the native savagery of the brute when irritated. If one can imagine the terror inspired by remorseless and unpitying fury,

* Bk. viii. ch. 17.   † Harl. MSS. 6085.

sudden and impetuous, we see its object fairly typified in the panther "incensed." The idea of fire and
smoke darting from its mouth, eyes and ears was
doubtless suggested by that habit peculiar to the
feline race, observable even in the domestic cat, to
"spit fire" and "swear" when rudely attacked, and
as an emblem in this sense it is extremely well indi-
cative of sudden fury.

Guillam says: "Some authors are of opinion that
there are no panthers bred in Europe; but in Africa,
Lybia and Mauritania they are plentiful. The
panther is a beast of a beautiful aspect, by reason of
the manifold variety of his divers coloured spots
wherewith his body is overspread. As a lion doth
in most things resemble the nature of a man, so,
after a sort, doth the panther of a woman; for it
is a beautiful beast, and fierce, yet very loving to
their young ones, and will defend them with the
hazard of their own lives; and if they miss them,
they bewail their loss with loud and miserable
howling."

The Lancastrian badge "the panther," says Planché,
"which is attributed by Sir William Segar to Henry
VI. and blazoned passant guardant argent spotted of
all colours with vapour issuant from her mouth and
ears; but there is no authority quoted for it, and
there is no example extant, the only collateral
evidence being the supporters of the Somerset Dukes
of Beaufort, who are supposed to have used it as a
token of their Lancastrian descent." The dexter

supporter of the Duke of Beaufort thus is blazoned : *Dexter, a panther argent, semée of torteaux, hurts and pomies alternately, flames issuant from the mouth and ears proper, gorged with a plain collar, and chained, or.*

The heraldic panther, or as it is more frequently termed, a panther incensed, is always borne *guardant, i.e.,* full-faced; and "incensed," that is to say, it is depicted with flames and smoke issuing from its mouth and ears. Its coat is spotted of various tinctures as the blazon may state.

Odet de Foix, Sieur de Lautrec, Marshal of France (+ 1528) being considered a person of fierce appearance, took for device a panther, with the motto "Allicit ulterius" ("He entices further"), alluding to the attractive power of that animal notwithstanding its fierce exterior, "an evidence," remarks a modern writer, "that he had as much vanity as ambition."

The town of Lucca for arms bears a panther : " *La pantera, che Lucca abbraccia e onora.*"

Gian Giacomo Trivulzio, surnamed the Great (+ 1518), a celebrated Italian soldier, bore a panther on his standard, with the motto, " Mens sibi conscia facti " ("The mind conscious to itself of the deed "), the panther signifying foresight (providence) from the number of eyes in his coat. Others said he wished to imply that he knew how to manage for himself in the various changes of his capricious fortune.*

* Hist. Dev. 260.

The Lynx.

The Lynx

Felis Lynx, or mountain cat, is found in the northern parts of Europe, Asia and America, and climbs the highest trees. He preys on squirrels, deer, hares, &c. He is fond of blood and kills great numbers of animals to satisfy his unconquerable thirst. He is smaller than the panther, about three feet and a half in length, his tail is much shorter and black at the extremity. His ears are erect with a pencil of black hair at the tips. The fur is long and thick, the upper part of the body is a pale grey, the under parts white.

The sight of the lynx is said to be so piercing that the ancients attributed to it the faculty of seeing through stone walls : it may, however, be asserted with truth that it distinguishes its prey at a greater distance than any other carnivorous quadruped. On this account it is frequently employed in heraldry, symbolising watchfulness, keenness of vision, and also the ability to profit by it.

Lynx-eyed, "oculis lynceis," originally referred to Lynceus, the argonaut, who was famed for the keenness of his vision ; then it was transferred to the lynx and gave rise to the fable that it could see through a wall (notes to "Philobiblon," by E. C. Thomas).

The Accademia de Lincei, founded in Rome in 1603, with the object of encouraging a taste for natural history, adopted the name and device of the lynx because the members should have the eyes of a lynx to penetrate the secrets of nature. Galileo, Fabio Colonna, and Gianbattista Porta were among the members of the academy, the latter philosopher and mathematician, who was the inventor of the camera obscura, bore the device of the academy, the lynx, and the motto " Aspicit et inspicit " (" Looks at and looks into ").

Charles IV. of Luxemburg, Emperor of Germany, adopted the lynx for his impress, with the motto, "Nullius pavit occursum " (" He fears not meeting with any one ").

THE LIZARD LYNX is an animal of the lynx or wild cat kind of a dark brown colour, spotted black ; the ears and tail are short. They are frequent in the woods of Sweden, Denmark and Norway, where they are usually termed lizards.

Cat-a-Mountain saliant, collared and lined.

Cat=a=Mountain—Tiger Cat or Wild Cat

THE Clan Chattan, who gave their name to the county of Caithness, bore as their cognisance the wild mountain cat, and called their chieftain, the Earl of Sutherland, " Mohr an chat " (The Great Wild Cat). The Mackintoshes still bear as their crests and supporters these ferocious cats, with the appropriate warning as a motto, " Touch not the cat but a glove." The whole is a pun upon the word " Catti," the Teutonic settlers of Caithness, *i.e.*, Catti-ness, and means " Touch not the Clan Cattan (or mountain cat) without a glove." Here " but " is used in the original meaning, beout, *i.e.*, without. For another example of "but" meaning without, see Amos iii. 7. The same words are also used as the motto of several Scottish families.

None will forget how the cat-a-mountain showed her claws to the Clan Kay, in the Wynds of Perth in Sir Walter Scott's "Fair Maid of Perth."

The Heraldic Musion.—Bossewell, in his work on heraldry published 1572, describes a musion as "a beaste that is enimie to myse and rattes." He adds also that he is "slye and wittie, and seeth so sharply, that he over-commeth darkness of the nighte by the shyninge lighte of his eyne. In the shape of body, he is like unto a leoparde, and hath a greate mouthe. He doth delighte that he enjoyeth his libertie, and in his youthe he is swifte, plyante, and merrie. He maketh a rufull noyse, and a gastefull when he proffereth to fighte with another. He is a cruel beaste when he is wilde and falleth on his owne feet from moste high places, and uneth (scarce) is hurte therewith. When he hathe a fayre skinne, he is, as it were, prowde thereof, and then he goeth fast aboute to be seene."

Crest, a Cat-a-Mountain, sejant, collared and lined.

Childebert, King of France, in token of his having

taken captive Gondomar of Bourgogne, assumed the device of a tiger-cat or ounce behind a grating or troillis, gules cloué argent.   This recalls the famous scene between Sanglier Rouge and Toison d'Or in " Quentin Durward," when Charles the Bold's jester professes to help the unhappy envoy of De la Marck by describing it as a cat looking out of a dairy window.

The cat, though domesticated, is considered as possessed of ingratitude; in its friendship so uncertain and so vicious in its nature, " that," say old writers, " it is only calculated for destroying the obnoxious race of rats and other small game."

From the mediæval superstition that Satan's favourite form was a black cat, it was superstitiously called "a familiar." Hence witches were said to have a cat as their familiar.

THE CAT : *A symbol of liberty.*—The Roman goddess of Liberty was represented as holding a cup in one hand, a broken sceptre in the other, and a cat lying at her feet.   No animal is so great an enemy to all constraint as a cat.

The cat was held in veneration by the Egyptians as sacred to the goddess Bubastis. This deity is represented with a human body and a cat's head. Diodorus tells us that whoever killed a cat, even by accident, was by the Egyptians punished with death. According to Egyptian tradition, Diana assumed the form of a cat, and thus excited the fury of the giants. The *London Review* says : "The Egyptians worshipped the cat as a symbol of the moon, not only because it is more active after sunset, but from the dilation and contraction of its orb, symbolical of the waxing and waning of the night goddess."

In heraldry it should always be represented full-faced like the leopard.

Erminois three cats-a-mountain passant gardant, in pale azure, each charged on the body with an ermine spot or. Crest : *a demi cat-a-mountain gardant, azure, gorged with a collar gemel, and charged with ermine spots, two and one.*—Tibbets.

The supporters of the Earl of Clanricarde are wild cats, and also those of the Earl of Belmore. It is the crest of De Burgh.

> " ÆNEAS.—His mantle was the lion's,
>   With all its tawny bars,
>   His falchion, like Orion's,
>   Was gemmed with golden stars.
>   Upon his lofty helmet
>   A brazen terror rode ;
>   No sword could overwhelm it
>   When in the fight it glowed.
>   For like a wild cat brindled,
>   It spat with eyes on fire,
>   And in the battle kindled
>   Immortal rage and ire,
>   Now in the sunshine sleeping,
>   How gently it reposed ;
>   But still in wisdom keeping
>   A single eye unclosed."
>
> *Queen Dido*, by T. S.

The Crowned Salamander of Francis I.

The Salamander

THE salamander has been immemorially credited
with certain fabulous powers. Less than a century
ago the creature was seriously described as a
"spotted lizard, which will endure the flames of
fire." Divested of its supernatural powers it is
simply a harmless little amphibian of the "newt"
family, from six to eight inches in length, with black
skin and yellow spots. The skin was long thought
to be poisonous, though it is in reality perfectly
harmless ; but the moist surface is so extremely
cold to the touch that, from this peculiar quality in
the creature, the idea must have arisen, not only that
it could withstand any heat to which it was exposed,
but it would actually subdue and put out fire.

This was a widespread belief long before the time

o

of Pliny, whose account of the creature is thus para-
phrased by Swift:

> " Further, we are by Pliny told
> This serpent is extremely cold ;
> So cold that, put it in the fire,
> 'Twill make the very flames expire."

Marco Polo, the early Venetian traveller, who tells
of many strange and wonderful things seen and
heard of in his journeyings, was not a believer in the
fabulous stories of the salamander, for he dismisses
the subject with the curt remark, " Everybody knows
that it could be no animal's nature to live in fire."
An early heraldic writer of a somewhat later period,
with greater credulity, stoutly maintains its reality,
and in describing the creature states that he actually
possessed some of the hair or down of the salamander. "This," he goes on to say, " I have
several times put in the fire and made it red-hot, and
after taken out ; which, being cold, yet remaineth
perfect wool, or fine downy hair."

Marco Polo further on assures his readers that the
true salamander is nothing but an incombustible substance found in the earth, " all the rest being fabulous
nonsense." He tells of a mountain in Tartary,
" there or thereabouts," in which a " vein " of salamander was found ; and so we arrive at the fact that
this salamander's wool was nothing but the "asbestos"
of the ancients. It is easy to see why asbestos became known as " salamanders' wool." The name

resulted from the juxtaposition of ideas, and shows how deeply impressed was the belief in the salamander's mysterious powers. A late writer tells us that some of the lizard tribe are known to enjoy warmth, and alligators are said to revel in hot water. It needed only that an insignificant member of the genus should have been found among the dead embers of a fire to prove at once the invulnerability of the reptile and its ability to extinguish the flames.

The salamander of mediæval superstition was a creature in the shape of a man, which lived in fire (Greek, salambeander, chimney-man), meaning a man that lives in a chimney. It was described by the ancients as bred by fire and existing in flames, an element which must inevitably prove destructive of life. Pliny describes it as "a sort of lizard which seeks the hottest fire to breed in, but quenches it with the extreme frigidity of its body." He tells us he tried the experiment once, but the creature was soon reduced to powder.*

Gregory of Nazianzen says that the salamander not only lived in and delighted in flames, but extinguished fire. St. Epiphanius compares the virtues of the hyacinth and the salamander. The hyacinth, he states, is unaffected by fire, and will even extinguish it as the salamander does. "The salamander and the hyacinth were symbols of enduring faith, which triumphs over the ardour of the passions.

* "Natural History," x. 67, xxix. 4.

Submitted to fire the hyacinth is discoloured and becomes white. We may here perceive," says M. Portal, "a symbol of enduring and triumphant faith."

This imaginary creature is generally represented as a small wingless dragon or lizard, surrounded by and breathing forth flames. Sometimes it is represented somewhat like a dog breathing flames. A

Salamander crest of James, Earl of Douglas.   From garter-plate.

golden salamander is so represented on the garter-plate of James, Earl of Douglas, K.G., the first Scottish noble elected into the Order of the Garter, and who died 1483 A.D. Tinctured *vert*; and *in flames proper* it is the crest of Douglas, Earl of Angus.

François I. of France adopted as his badge the salamander in the midst of flames, with the legend, " Nutrisco et extinguo " ("I nourish and extinguish"). The Italian motto from which this legend was borrowed was, " Nudrisco il buono e spengo il reo " (" I nourish the good and extinguish the bad ; " " Fire purifies good metal, but consumes rubbish "). In his castle of Chambord, the galleries of the Palace

of Fontainebleau, and the Hôtel St. Bourg Thoroulde
at Rouen, this favourite device of the crowned salamander, with the motto, may be everywhere seen.

Azure, a salamander or, in flames proper, is the
charge on the shield of the Italian family of Cennio.

The " *lizards* " which form the crest of the Ironmongers' Company, were probably intended for salamanders on the old seal of the company in 1483,
but are now blazoned as lizards.

The heraldic signification of the salamander was
that of a brave and generous courage that the fire of
affliction cannot destroy or consume.

In the animal symbolism of the ancients the salamander may be said to represent the element of
FIRE; the eagle, AIR ; the lion, EARTH ; the
dolphin, WATER.

Heraldic Antelope

THIS fictitious animal, when depicted in heraldry,
has a body like that of a stag, the tail of a unicorn, a head like the heraldic tiger, with two
serrated horns, and a tusk growing from the tip of
his nose, a row of tufts down the back of his neck,
and the like on his tail, chest and thighs. Thus
represented it is termed an heraldic antelope to distinguish it from the real or natural antelope, which
is also borne in modern coats of arms.

The old heralds, with their scant knowledge of

the rarer kinds of foreign animals, represented the antelope as a fierce beast of prey, and totally unlike in appearance and in disposition to the beautiful small-limbed gentle creature with which we are acquainted. That such was the prevailing opinion

Heraldic Antelope.

in the time of Spenser is evident. In the "Faerie Queen" he makes the stout Sir Satyrane—

"In life and manners wild,
Amongst wild beasts and woods from laws of man exiled."

—more than a match for the most ferocious brutes, all of whom he subdues :

"Wild beasts in iron yokes he would compel ;
The spotted panther, and the tuskèd boar ;

The pardale swift, and the tiger cruel,
The *antelope* and wolf, both fierce and fell ;
And them constrain in equal team to draw."

Some authorities give the heraldic antelope with two straight horns, but as the ancient badge of the House of Lancaster it was represented with two serrated horns curving backward.

In blazon, the term " *heraldic antelope* " should always be used unless the natural antelope is intended.

The Heraldic Ibex

is an imaginary beast resembling the heraldic antelope in appearance, with the exception of the horns projecting from his forehead, which are serrated like a saw. Perhaps it would not be erroneous to consider it identical with the heraldic antelope.

The real or natural ibex is a native of the Alps, the Pyrenees and the Grecian mountains, where they abound in defiance of the hunters. It resembles a goat, but the horns are much larger, bent backwards, and full of knots, one of which is added every year.

The Heraldic Ibex.

Bagwyn

A FABULOUS beast like the heraldic antelope, but having the tail of a horse, and long horns of a goat curved backwards. The dexter supporter of the arms of Carey, Lord Hundson, in Westminster Abbey, is a Bagwyn.

The Camelopard, Camel-leopard

THE Giraffe figures a few times in blazon under these names. It is described by old heralds as half camel and half leopard. A curious word-combination was made by the Romans when wishing to find a name for the giraffe. "It is," says Archbishop Trench, "a creature combining, though with infinitely more grace, yet some of the height and even the proportions of *a camel*, with the spotted skin of the *pard*." They called it "camelopardus," the camel-panther.

There are two heraldic creatures based upon the above which are referred to in heraldic works, viz., the ALLOCAMELUS or ass-camel, having the body of the camel conjoined to the head of an ass ; and the CAMELOPARDEL, which is like the camelopard, but with two long horns curved backwards.

Musimon, Tityrus

A FICTITIOUS animal mentioned by Guillim and
others. It nearly re-
sembles *a goat, with the
head and horns of a ram*,
but has besides the horns
of that beast, *pair of
goat's horns.* is also
mentioned in Guillim's
"Display," w re it is
said to be a igenerous
beast, of unkindly pro-
creation, engendered be-
tween a goat and a ram,
like the Tityrus, the offspring of a sheep and
goat, as noted by Upton.

Musimon, Tityrus.

The Enfield

AN imaginary hybrid animal with *the head of a
fox, chest of a greyhound, talons of an eagle, and body
of a lion ; the hind legs and tail of a wolf.* It occurs
as the crest of some Irish families of the name of
Kelly.

Mantygre—Satyral.

Mantiger, Montegre or Manticora
Satyral

A CHIMERICAL creature of mediæval invention, having the body of an heraldic tiger with mane, and the head of an old man with long spiral horns. Some heraldic authorities make the horns more like those of an ox, and the feet like a dragon's.

The Satyral is apparently identical with the man-tiger.

The belief that certain persons have the power of assuming the shape of the tiger is common in India, and the Khonds say that a man-killing tiger is either an incarnation of the Earth's goddess or a transfigured man. It is thus with the Lavas of Birma, supposed to be the broken-down remains of a cultured race and dreaded as man-tigers.*

Two satyrals supported the arms of the Lords Stawell.

The supporters of the arms of the Earl of Huntingdon are mantigers, but are represented without horns.

From a mediæval " Bestiaria " we have a description and illustration of a gruesome creature of this name (manticora), evolved no doubt from some traveller's marvellous tale. We are told that it is " bred among the Indians," has a triple row of teeth, in bigness and roughness like a lion's, face and ears like a man's, a tail like a scorpion's " with a sting and sharp-pointed quills," and that " his voice is like a small trumpet," and that he is " very wild," and that after having his tail bruised, he can be tamed without danger.

Manticora.   From ancient Bestiaria.

There are several other fictitious creatures, which, if we may believe certain old writers, excited the minds of our credulous wonder-loving forefathers. Of these little need be said, as they rarely, if ever, appear in modern works on heraldry, and may therefore be classed as extinct monsters.

* Tylor's " Primitive Culture."

Lamia or Emipusa

A curious creature of the imagination is the lamia, of which we are told many fictitious stories. It is said

Lamia. From old Bestiary.

to be " the swiftest of all four-footed creatures, that it is very treacherous and cruel to men. It is stated to be bred in Lybia, and sometimes devours its own young." It is represented in an ancient " Bestiaria " as having the head and breasts of a woman, and the body of a four-footed animal with flowing tail, the hind feet having divided hoofs. It is " thought to be the creature mentioned in Isaiah xxxiv., called in Hebrew *Lilith*, as also the same which is mentioned in Lamentations iv."

In Dr. Brewer's "Dictionary of Phrase and Fable," Lamia is " a female phantom whose name was used by the Greeks and Romans as a bugbear to children, from the classic fable of a Lybian Queen beloved by Jupiter, but robbed of her children by Juno ; and in consequence she vowed vengeance against all children, whom she delighted to entice and murder." They are again described as spectres of Africa, who attracted strangers and then devoured them. In the story of " Machatës and Philemon," a young man is represented as marrying an Empusa, who sucks his blood at night. Goethe borrowed his ballad of the " Bride of Corinth " from this tale.

Beyond casual mention this mythical creature does not appear in heraldry.

Baphomet

A FICTITIOUS creature having two heads, male and female, the rest of the body female ; said to be used as an idol or symbol by the Templars in their mysterious rites. The word is a corruption of Mahomet. Though mentioned in old works it does not now appear in British heraldry.

Apres

A FICTITIOUS animal resembling a bull, with a short tail like that of a bear. It is the sinister supporter of the arms of the Company of Muscovy Merchants.

Stelliones

THE supporters of the Ironmongers' Company of London are two lizards. Bossewell describes beasts of similar shape—" Stelliones " as he terms them, evidently in allusion to steel. He says, " Stellio is a beaste like a lysard, having on his back spotts like starres."*

Stellione-serpent, a serpent with the head of a weasel, borne by the name of Baume.

* Armorie of Honour, 62.

Fictitious Creatures of the Sea

INTRODUCTORY NOTES

" The sea, that is
A world of waters heapèd up on high,
Rolling like mountains in wild wilderness,
Horrible, hideous, roaring with hoarse cry !"

SPENSER.

" I can call spirits from the vasty deep."

SHAKESPEARE.

ARINERS in all ages, prone to superstitious fears, have peopled the great deep with beings of the most dreadful kind, all the more wonderful and indescribable because of the mysterious and unknown regions in the sea depths which they were supposed to inhabit. Classic mythology in its wealth of imagery allotted a whole hierarchy of greater and lesser divinities to the government of the watery element, whose capricious ruling of the waves man altogether failed to comprehend. Their fancied terrors, begot in calms and storms, in darkness and in fogs, midst dangers of the most appalling kind, assumed those monstrous and fantastic shapes which their own fears created. The active forces of nature in unusual

P

forms impressed them as the result of supernatural
agency, or the "meddling of the gods," whose
favours and protection the mariner, by prayers and
supplications, endeavoured to propitiate ; and whilst
tremblingly he skirts the horizon's edge in timid ventures, new dangers impel him to promises of greater
gifts to assuage the wrathful mood of his angry god
or some other equally powerful or more spiteful.

The national god of the Philistines was represented
with the face and hands of a man and the tail of a
fish.   It was but natural that a seafaring people should
adopt a god of that form.

> " Dagon his name ; sea-monster, upward man
> And downward fish : yet had his temple high
> Reared in Azotus, dreaded through the coast
> Of Palestine, in Gath and Ascalon,
> And Accaron and Gaza's frontier bounds."
>
> *Paradise Lost*, Book i. 462.

In the leviathan and behemoth of Scripture are
darkly indicated monsters of the great deep.   Scandinavian mythology, like that of all bold maritime
peoples in old times, is rife with legends of
certain great monsters of the sea.   The kraken or
sea-serpent of popular legend is a myth not yet laid
to rest ; there is still a lingering belief in the existence
of the mermaid.

> " With a comb and a glass in her hand, her hand, her hand,
> With a comb and a glass in her hand."
>
> Popular sea-song.

Chief amongst the Grecian sea-divinities stands *Poseidon*, or *Neptune* as he was called by the Romans, the potent " ruler of the seas." He usually dwelt, not in Olympus, but at the bottom of the sea, in a magnificent golden palace in the neighbourhood of Ægæ. He is always represented with a trident, sometimes with a rudder—special symbols of his power over the sea. Accompanied by his wife, fair Amphitrite, he was frequently pictured in royal state in his chariot, drawn through the billows by wild sea-horses, attended by "Triton blowing loud his wreathed horn," Proteus, "the godlike shepherd of the sea," and other followers—dolphins leaping the waves and showing their high arched backs in wild gambolings.

Nereus and his fifty daughters, the *Nereides*, who dwelt in caves and grottos of the ocean—beneficent sea-nymphs,—win the hearts of the sailors, now by their merry sports and dances, now by their timely assistance in the hour of danger. Whilst Nereus and his lovely daughters represent the sea under its calm and pleasant aspect, Thaumas, Phorcys, Ceto present it as the world of wonders, under its more terrible conditions. The storm winds and all the terrors and dangers of the deep were typified under various strange and peculiar forms. Not the least dreaded were the *Sirens*, fatal sisters, who "spread o'er the silver waves their golden hair," basked near sunlit rocks, and lured all men to their ruin by their enchanting voices, save only the crafty Ulysses.

These and many others of lesser note, Proteus, Glaucus and the rest, make up the discordant influences that govern the watery element.

Many wonderful stories are told by classic writers concerning these old myths, and innumerable relics of antique art which embody the conceptions of the times are extant in our museums, by which we may judge to what a large extent such ideas influenced the common life and formed the beliefs of ancient peoples.

It is also worthy of observation to note in what manner the ancients sought to identify the various sea-deities and other mythical creatures with the element they lived in. Each was known by his form or the attributes by which he was accompanied. Modern heraldry repeats many of these old-world myths as new-coined fables, so that for their proper understanding and signification it will be necessary briefly to refer to ancient ideas respecting them. Lakes, rivers and fountains had each their impersonation peculiar to them, which will be found referred to in classic story.

Mediæval legend is equally rife with accounts of wonderful creatures of the sea. The change of one form of superstition for another alters but little the constitution of the mind to harbour fears, and the imagination will deceive even the wisest and best so long as Nature's laws are misunderstood.

Particular whirlpools, rocks and other dangerous places to navigation, are personated under the forms

of monsters of various and awful shapes feared by
the mariner, who dreads

"The loud yell of watery wolves to hear."

Scylla and Charybdis are two rocks which lie
between Italy and Sicily. Ships which tried to avoid
one were often wrecked on the other. The ancients
feigned an interesting legend to account for their
existence. It was Circe who changed Scylla into a
frightful sea monster, and Jupiter who changed
Charybdis into a whirlpool, the noise of which was
likened to the loud barking of dogs ; and the monster
was therefore represented with savage dogs amidst
her scaly folds, and loudly baying.

> " Far on the right her dogs foul Scylla hides;
> Charybdis roaring on the left presides,
> And in her greedy whirlpool sucks the tides,
> Then spouts them from below ; with fury driven
> The waves mount up, and wash the face of heaven.
> But Scylla from her den with open jaws
> The sinking vessel in her eddy draws
> Then dashes on the rocks. A human face
> And virgin bosom hides her tail's disgrace ;
> Her parts obscene below the waves descend,
> With dogs enclosed, and in a dolphin end."
>
> *Æneid*, Book iii.

Homer gives a vivid description of Ulysses passing
the rocks and whirlpools :

> " Now through the rocks, appall'd with deep dismay,
> We bend our course, and stem the desperate way ;

Dire Scylla there a scene of horror forms ;
And here Charybdis fills the deep with storms.
When the tide rushes from her rumbling caves,
The rough rock roars, tumultuous boil the waves ;
They toss, they foam, a wild confusion raise,
Like water bubbling o'er the fiery blaze ;
Eternal mists obscure the aërial plain,
And high across the rocks she spouts the main :
When in her gulfs the rushing sea subsides,
She drains the ocean with the refluent tides :
The rock rebellows with a thundering sound ;
Deep, wondrous deep, below appears the ground."

Odyssey, Book xii.

The giants and ogres of romance were never so fearfully armed or clothed by the wildest fiction with so terrible an aspect as the cephalopods, the race to which the cuttlefish or octopus belongs. Eminently carnivorous, voracious and fierce ; beneath staring eyes are spread eight strong fleshy arms furnished with tenacious suckers, which adhere with unrelenting pertinacity, and the arms are swiftly twined round the struggling prey, which vainly strives to disengage itself from so fearful and so fatal embrace. Cephalopods of enormous size are sometimes found with arms as thick as a man's thigh. Homer refers to its tenacity of grip in a simile.

The cuttlefish appears upon ancient Greek coins of Coressus, in allusion to the worship of Neptune, a deity much venerated as the protector of this island.

Amongst the veritable inhabitants of the ocean there are few more extraordinary mammals than the sea-unicorn, *Monodon monoceros*, the beaked whale of the Arctic seas, twenty to thirty feet from stern to snout. His length is increased about eight feet by his magnificent spirally twisted tusk of the purest ivory, which in reality is simply the canine tooth growing straight out of the upper jaw. One of the royal treasures of Denmark is the narwhal throne of the Castle of Rosenberg. It is the horn of this "strange fish" which has kept up the belief in the existence of the mythical unicorn.

Xiphias gladius, swordfish, is the largest of the thorny fishes, and belongs to the scombers or mackerel group. The sawfish, *Pristis antiquorum,* ranks by himself between the rays and sharks. He has the long body of a shark and the underside gill openings of a ray. His saw, like the sword of the Xiphias, is a long flattened bony snout, but is double-edged and serrated. It is well known as a weapon among the Polynesian islanders, and, like the sword of the Xiphias, is frequently found buried in the hulls of ocean-going ships.

There are two denizens of the deep which bear the name of sea-horse—one the tiny Hippocampus, the other the mighty walrus. The hippocampus of our public aquariums, a bony pipefish some six or eight inches in length, swimming upright, his favourite position in the water, with the general resemblance of his head to that of a horse, is very striking; anchored to the seaweed stems by their tails they dart on their prey with great quickness.

Hippocampus (ἴππος, *hippos*, a horse ; κάμπη, *campe*, a bending), the steed of Neptune, had only the two forelegs of a horse, the hinder quarter being that of a dolphin.   The word means " coiling horse."

The Sea-horse of the North, or walrus—the *Ross-mareus* or *Morse* of the Scandinavians, the *Trichecus rosmarus* of science, is fifteen or twenty feet long, or even longer, and armed with huge canine teeth, sometimes measuring thirty inches in length—tusks which furnish no small amount of our commercial ivory.   Many are the thrilling stories of the chase of these great sea-horses, for the walrus fights for his life as determinedly as any animal hunted by man. The walrus has had the honour assigned to it also of being the original of the mermaid, and Scoresby says the front part of the head of a young one without tusks might easily be taken at a little distance for a human face, especially as it has a habit of raising its head straight out of the water to look at passing ships.

The manatee, or sea-cow, found on the tropical coasts and streams of Africa and America, is called by the Portuguese and Spaniards the " woman-fish," from its supposed close resemblance.   Its English name comes from the flipper resembling a human hand—*manus*—with which it holds its young to its breast.   One of this species, which died at the Royal Aquarium in 1878, was as unlike the typical mermaid as one could possibly imagine, giving one a very startling idea of the difference between romance and reality ; but if it was observed in its native haunts, and seen at some little distance, and then only by glimpses, it might possibly, as some have asserted, present a very striking resemblance to the human form.

Sir James Emerson Tennent, speaking of the *Dugong*, an herbivorous cetacean, says its head has a rude approach to the human outline, and the mother while suckling her young holds it to her breast with one flipper, as a woman holds an infant in her arm ; if disturbed she suddenly dives under water and throws up her fish-like tail.   It is this creature, he says, which has probably given rise to the tales about mermaids.

Seals differ from all other animals in having the toes of the feet included almost to the end in a common integument, converting them into broad fins armed with strong non-retractile claws.   Of the many varieties of the seal family, from Kamchatka comes the noisy " SEA-LION " (*Otaria jubata*), so called from his curious mane.   In the same neighbourhood we get the " SEA-LEOPARD " (*Leptonyx weddellii*), and the " SEA-BEAR " (the *Etocephalus ursinus*), whose larger and better-developed limbs enable him to stand and walk on shore.   But the most important of the seals, in a commercial sense, are the " HARP SEAL " (*Phoca Grœnlandica*) and the COMMON SEAL, or " SEA-DOG " (*Phoca vitulina*), which yield the skins so valuable to the furrier.   There are several other species, of which the most known are the CRESTED SEAL, or *Neistsersoak* (*Stemmatopus cristatus*), and the BEARDED SEAL (*Phoca barbata*).

Apart from the seal having possibly given rise to legends of the mermaid, it has a distinguished position in superstition and mythology on its own account. In Shetland it is the "haff-fish," or selkie, a fallen spirit. Evil is sure to follow the unfortunate destroyer of one of these creatures. In the Faroe Islands there is a superstition that the seals cast off their skins every ninth night and appear as mortals, dancing until daybreak on the sands. Sometimes they are induced to marry, but if ever they recover their skins they betake themselves again to the water.

Stephen of Byzantium relates that the ships of certain Greek colonists were on their expeditions followed by an immense number of seals, and it was probably on this account that the city they founded in Asia received the name of Phocea, from φώκη (*Phoké*), the Greek name of a seal, and they also adopted that animal as the type or badge of the city upon their coinage. The gold pieces of the Phoceans were well known among the Greek States, and are frequently referred to by ancient writers. "Thus from a single coin," says Noel Humphreys,* "we obtain the corroboration of the legend of the swarm of seals, of the remote epoch of the emigration in question, the coin being evidently of the earliest period, most probably of the middle of the seventh century before the Christian era."

Luigi (+ 1598), brother to the Duke of Mantua, had for device a seal asleep upon a rock in a troubled

* "Coin Collector's Manual," Bohn.

sea, with the motto: "Sic quiesco" ("So rest I"). The seal, say the ancient writers, is never struck by lightning. The Emperor Augustus always wore a belt of seal-skin. "There is no living creature sleepeth more soundly," says Pliny,* "therefore when storms arise and the sea is rough the seal goes upon the rocks where it sleeps in safety unconscious of the storm."

The poet Spenser embodies many of the conceptions of his time in the description of the crowning adventures of the Knight Guyon. He here refers to "great sea monsters of all ugly shapes and horrible aspects" "such as Dame Nature's self might fear to see."

> "Spring-headed hydras, and sea-shouldering whales ;
> Great whirlpools, which all fishes make to flee ;
> Bright scolopendras arm'd with silver scales ;
> Mighty monoceroses with unmeasured tails ;
>
> The dreadful fish that hath deserved the name
> Of death, and like him looks in dreadful hue ;
> The grisly wasserman, that makes his game
> The flying ships with swiftness to pursue ;
>
> The horrible sea-satyr that doth shew
> His fearful face in time of greatest storm ;
> Huge Ziffius, whom mariners eschew
> No less than rocks, as travellers inform ;
> And greedy rose-marines with visages deform ;
> All these, and thousand thousand many more
> And more deformed monsters, thousandfold."
>
> *Faerie Queen*, Book ii. cant. xii.

---

* Book ix. ch. 13.

The early heralds took little account of these dreadful creatures—more easily imagined by fearful mariners or by poets than depicted by artists from their vague descriptions. The most imaginative of the tribe rarely ventured beyond such representations of marine monsters as appealed strongly and clearly to the universal sense of mankind—compounds of marine and land animals—either from a belief in the existence of such creatures, or because they used them as emblems or types of qualities, combining for this purpose the attributes of certain inhabitants of the sea with those of the land or of the air to form the appropriate symbol.

In modern heraldry such bearings are usually adopted with special allusion to actions performed at sea, or they have reference in some way to the name or designation of the bearer, and hence termed allusive or canting heraldry. Some maritime towns bear nautical devices of the fictitious kind referred to. For instance, the City of Liverpool has for supporters Neptune with his trident, and a Triton with his horn. Cambridge and Newcastle-on-Tyne have sea-horses for supporters to their city's arms. Belfast has the sea-horse for sinister supporter and also for crest.

Many of the nobility also bear, either as arms or supporters, these mythical sea creatures, pointing in many instances to memorable events in their family history ; indeed, as islanders and Britons, marine emblems—real and mythical—enter largely into our national heraldry.

Poseidon or Neptune

POSEIDON or Neptune, the younger brother of Zeus (Jupiter), sometimes appears in heraldry, usually as a supporter. In the ancient mythology he was origin- ally a mere symbol of the watery element, he after- wards became a distinct personality ; the mighty ruler of the sea who with his powerful arms upholds and circumscribes the earth, violent and impetu- ous like the element he represents. When he strikes the sea with his trident, the symbol of his sovereignty, the waves rise with vio- lence, as a word or look from him suffices to allay the fiercest tem- pest. Poseidon (Nep- tune) was naturally

Dexter supporter of Baron Hawke.

regarded as the chief patron and tutelary deity of the seafaring Greeks. To him they addressed their prayers before entering on a voyage, and to him they

brought their offerings in gratitude for their safe
return from the perils of the deep.

In a famous episode of the " Faerie Queen " (Book
iv. c. xi.) Spenser glowingly pictures the procession
of all the water deities and their attendants :

> " First came great Neptune with his three-forked mace,
>   That rules the seas and makes them rise and fall ;
>   His dewy locks did drop with brine apace
>   Under his diadem imperial :

> " And by his side his Queen with coronal,
>   Fair Amphitrite, most divinely fair,
>   Whose ivory shoulders weren covered all,
>   As with a robe, with her own silver hair,
>   And decked with pearls which the Indian seas for her
>   prepare."

Amphitrite, his wife, one of the Nereids in ancient
art, is represented as a slim and beautiful young
woman, her hair falling loosely about her shoulders,
and distinguished from all the other deities by the
royal insignia. On ancient coins and gems she
appears enthroned on the back of a mighty triton,
or riding on a sea-horse, or dolphin.

EXAMPLES.—Baron Hawke bears for supporters
to his shield an aggroupment of classic personations
of a remarkable symbolic character, granted for the
achievements of the renowned Admiral and Com-
mander-in-Chief of the Fleet, Vice-Admiral of Great
Britain, &c. &c., created Baron Hawke of Tarton,
Yorks, 1776. *The dexter supporter is a figure of*

Neptune, his mantle vert, edged argent, crowned with an
eastern crown, or, his dexter arm erect and holding a trident
pointing downwards in the act of striking, sable, headea
silver, and resting his left foot on a dolphin proper.
Sir Isaac Heard, Somersetshire ; Lancaster Herald,
afterwards Garter.   His arms, granted 1762, are
thus blazoned in Burke's " General Armory " :
Argent a Neptune crowned with an eastern crown of
gold, his trident sable headed or, issuing from a stormy
ocean, the sinister hand grasping the head of a ship's
mast appearing above the waves, as part of a wreck, all
proper ; on a chief azure, the Arctic pole-star of the first
between two water-bougets of the second.

Merman or Triton

" *Triton, who boasts his high Neptunian race*
  Sprung from the God by Salace's embrace."
                              CAMOËNS, " Lusiad."

" *Triton his trumpet shrill before them blew*
  For goodly triumph and great jolliment
  That made the rocks to roar as they were rent."
                              SPENSER, " Faerie Queen."
                        (Procession of the Sea Deities.)

TRITON was the only son of Neptune and Amphitrite.   The poet Apollonius Rhodius describes him
as having the upper parts of the body of a man,
while the lower parts were those of a dolphin.

Later poets and artists revelled in the conception of a whole race of similar tritons, who were re-

Merman or Triton.

garded as a wanton, mischievous tribe, like the satyrs on land. Glaucus, another of the inferior deities, is represented as a triton, rough and shaggy in appearance, his body covered with mussels and seaweed ; his hair and beard show that luxuriance which characterises sea-gods. Proteus, as shepherd of the seas, is usually distinguished with a crook. Triton, as herald of Neptune, is represented always holding, or blowing, his wreathed horn or conch shell. His mythical duties as attendant on the supreme sea-divinity

Triton, with two tails.   German.

would, as an emblem in heraldry, imply a similar duty or office in the bearer to a great naval hero.

EXAMPLES.—The City of Liverpool has for sinister supporter a *Triton blowing a conch shell and holding a flag in his right hand.*

Mermaid and Triton supporters.

Lord Lyttelton bears for supporters *two Mermen proper, in their exterior hands a trident or.*

Ottway, Bart.—Supporters on either side, *a Triton blowing his shell proper, navally crowned or, across the shoulder a wreath of red coral, and holding in the exterior hand a trident, point downward.*

Note.—In classic story, Triton and the Siren are distinct poetic creations, their vocation and attributes

Q

being altogether at variance—no relationship whatever existing between them. According to modern popular notions, however, the siren or mermaid, and triton, or merman as they sometimes term him, appear to be viewed as male and female of the same creature (in heraldic parlance baron and femme). They thus appear in companionship as supporters to the arms of Viscount Hood, and similarly in other achievements.

The Mermaid or Siren

" Mermaid shapes that still the waves with ecstasies of song."
T. SWAN,
" The World within the Ocean."

" And fair Ligea's golden comb,
Wherewith she sits on diamond rocks,
Sleeking her soft alluring hair."
MILTON, " Comus."

THIS fabulous creature of the sea, well known in ancient and modern times as the frequent theme of poets and the subject of numberless legends, has from a very early date been a favourite device. She is usually represented in heraldry as having the upper part the head and body of a beautiful young woman, holding a comb and glass in her hands, the lower part ending in a fish.

Ellis (Glasfryn, Merioneth).—*Argent, a mermaid gules, crined or, holding a mirror in her right hand and a comb in her left, gold. Crest, a mermaid as in the arms. Motto,* " Worth ein ffrwythau yn hadna byddir." Another family of the same name, settled in Lancashire, bears the colours reversed, viz., *gules, a mermaid argent.*

Sir Josiah Mason.—Crest, *a mermaid, per fess wavy argent and azure, the upper part guttée de larmes,* in the dexter hand a comb, and in the sinister a mirror, frame and hair sable.

Crest of Ellis.

Balfour of Burleigh.—*On a rock, a mermaid proper, holding in her dexter hand an otter's head erased sable, and in the sinister a swan's head, erased proper.* The supporters of Baron Balfour are an otter and a swan, which will account for the heads appearing in the hands of the mermaid, instead of the traditionary comb and mirror. In some other instances the like occurs, as in the mermaid crest of Cussack, *the mermaid sable crined or, holds in dexter hand a sword, and in the sinister a sceptre.*

Sir George Francis Bonham, Bart.—*Crest, a mermaid holding in dexter hand a wreath of coral, and in the sinister a mirror.*

Wallop, Earl of Portsmouth, bears for crest *a mermaid proper,* with her usual accompaniments, the comb and mirror. Another family of the same name and bearing the same arms has for crest *a mermaid with two tails extended proper, hair gold, holding her tails in her hands extended wide.*

In foreign heraldry the mermaid is generally termed *Mélusine*, and represented with two fishy extremities.

Die Ritter, of Nuremberg bears *per fess sable and or, a mermaid holding her two tails, vested gules, crowned or.*

Die Ritter, of Nuremberg.

The Austrian family of Estenberger bears for crest *a mermaid without arms, and having wings.*

A mermaid was the device of Sir William de Brivere, who died in 1226. It is the badge of the Berkeleys ; in the monumental brass of Lord Berkeley, at Wolton-under-Edge, 1392 A.D., he bears a collar of mermaids over his camail. `The Black Prince, in his will, mentions certain devices that he appears to have used as badges ; among the rest we find " Mermaids of the Sea." It was the dexter supporter in the coat-of-arms of Sir Walter Scott, and the crest of Lord Byron. The supporters of Viscount Boyne are mermaids. Skiffington, Viscount Marsereene, the Earl of Caledon, the Earl of Howth, Viscount Hood, and many other titled families bear it as crest or supporters. It is also borne by many untitled families.

The arms of the princely house of Lusignan, kings of Cyprus and Jerusalem, " Une sirène dans une cuvé," were founded on a curious mediæval legend of a mermaid or siren, termed Mélusine, a fairy, condemned by some spell to become on one day of the week only, half woman, half serpent. The Knight Roimoudin de Forez, meeting her in the forest by chance, became enamoured and married her, and she became the mother of several children, but she carefully avoided seeing her husband on the day of her change ; one day, however, his curiosity led him to watch her, which led to the spell being broken, and the soul with which by her union with a Christian she hoped to have been endowed, was lost to her for ever.

This interesting myth is fully examined in Baring Gould's " Curious Myths of the Middle Ages."

The mermaid is represented as the upper half of a beautiful maiden joined to the lower half of a fish, and usually holding a comb in the right hand and a mirror in the left; these articles of the toilet have reference to the old fable that always when observed by man mermaids are found to be resting upon the waves, combing out their long yellow hair, while admiring themselves in the glass : they are also accredited with wondrous vocal powers, to hear which was death to the listener. It was long believed such creatures really did exist, and had from time to time been seen and spoken with ; many, we are told, have fatally listened to " the mermaid's charmèd speech," and have blindly followed the beguiling, deluding creature to her haunts beneath the wave, as did Sidratta, who, falling in the Ganges, became enamoured of one of these beautiful beings, the Upsaras, the swan-maidens of the Vedas.

All countries seem to have invented some fairy-like story of the waters. The Finnish Nakki play their silver harps o' nights ; the water imp or Nixey of Germany sings and dances on land with mortals, and the " Davy " (Deva), whose " locker " is at the bottom of the deep blue sea, are all poetical conceptions of the same description. The same may be said of the Merminne of the Netherlands, the White Lady of Scotland and the Silver Swan of the German legend, that drew the ship in which the Knight Lohengrin departed never to return.

In the " Bestiary " of Philip de Thaun he tells us that " Siren lives in the sea, it sings at the approach of a storm and weeps in fine weather ; such is its nature : and it has the make of a woman down to the waist, and the feet of a falcon, and the tail of a fish. When it will divert itself, then it sings loud and clear ; if then the steersman who navigates the sea hears it, he forgets his ship and immediately falls asleep."

The legendary mermaid still retains her place in popular legends of our sea coasts, especially in the remoter parts of our islands. The stories of the Mirrow, or Irish fairy, hold a prominent place among Crofton Croker's " Fairy Legends of the South of Ireland." Round the shores of Lough Neagh old people still tell how, in the days of their youth, mermaids were supposed to reside in the water, and with what fear and trepidation they would, on their homeward way in the twilight, approach some lonely and sequestered spot on the shore, expecting every moment to be captured and carried off by the witching mere-maidens. On the Continent the same idea prevails. Among the numerous legends of the Rhine many have reference to the same fabled creature.

As we know, mariners in all ages have delighted in tales of the marvellous, and in less enlightened times than the present, they were not unlikely to have found many willing listeners and sound believers. Early voyagers tell wonderful stories of these "fish-women," or "women-fish," as they termed them. The ancient chronicles indeed teem with tales of the capture of "mermaids," "mermen," and similar strange creatures; stories which now only excite a smile from their utter absurdity. So late as 1857 there appeared an article in the *Shipping Gazette*, under intelligence of June 4, signed by some Scotch sailors, and describing an object seen off the North British coast "in the shape of a woman, with full breast, dark complexion, comely face" and the rest. It is probable that some variety of the seal family may be the prototype of this interesting myth.

The myth of the mermaid is, however, of far older date; Homer and later Greek and Roman poets have said and sung a great deal about it.

The Sirens of Classic Mythology

THE SIRENS (Greek, entanglers) enticed seamen by the sweetness of their song to such a degree that the listeners forgot everything and died of hunger. Their names were, Parthenope, Ligea, and Leucosia.

Parthenope, the ancient name of Neapolis (Naples)

Ulysses and the Sirens. Flaxman's "Odyssey."

was derived from one of the sirens, whose tomb was shown in Strabo's time. Poetic legend states that she threw herself into the sea out of love for Ulysses, and was cast up on the Bay of Naples.

The celebrated Parthenon at Athens, the beautiful temple of Pallas Athenæ, so richly adorned with sculptures, likewise derives its name from this source.

Dante interviews the siren in "Purgatorio," xix. 7–33.

Flaxman, in his designs illustrating the "Odyssey," represents the sirens as beautiful young women seated on the strand and singing.

In the illustration from an ancient Greek vase

Ulysses and the Sirens.   From a painting on a Greek vase.

gives a Grecian rendering of the story, and represents the Sirens as birds with heads of maidens.

The Sirens are best known from the story that Odysseus succeeded in passing them with his companions without being seduced by their song. He had the prudence to stop the ears of his companions with wax and to have himself bound to the mast.   Only two are mentioned in Homer, but three or four are mentioned in later times and introduced into various legends.   Demeter (*Ceres*)

is said to have changed their bodies into those
of birds, because they refused to go to the help of
their companion, Persephone, when she was carried
off by Pluto. " They are represented in Greek art
like the harpies, as young women with the wings and
feet of birds. Sometimes they appear altogether like
birds, only with human faces; at other times with the
bodies of women, in which case they generally hold
instruments of music in their hands. As their songs
are death to those subdued by them they are often
depicted on tombs as spirits of death."

By the fables of the Sirens is represented the en-
snaring nature of vain and deceitful pleasures, which
sing and soothe to sleep, and never fail to destroy
those who succumb to their beguiling influence.

Spenser, in the " Faerie Queen," describes a place
"where many mermaids haunt, making false melodies,"
by which the knight Guyon makes a somewhat
" perilous passage." There were five sisters that had
been fair ladies, till too confident in their skill in
music they had ventured to contend with the Muses,
when they were transformed in their lower extremities
to fish :

> " But the upper half their hue retained still,
> And their sweet skill in wonted melody ;
> Which ever after they abused to ill
> To allure weak travellers, whom gotten they did kill."
> Book ii. cant. cxii.

Shakespeare charmingly pictures Oberon in the
moonlight, fascinated by the graceful form and the

melodious strains of the mermaid half reclining on the back of the dolphin :

> " OBERON : . . . Thou rememberest
> Since once I sat upon a promontory,
> And heard a mermaid on a dolphin's back
> Uttering such dulcet and harmonious breath
> That the rude sea grew civil at her song
> And certain stars shot madly from their spheres
> To hear the sea-maid's music."

Commentators of Shakespeare find in this passage (and subsequent parts) certain references to Mary Queen of Scots, which they consider beyond dispute. She was frequently referred to in the poetry of the time under this title. She was married to the Dauphin (or Dolphin) of France. The rude sea means the Scotch rebels, and the shooting stars referred to were the Earls of Northumberland and Westmoreland, who, with others of lesser note, forgot their allegiance to Elizabeth out of love to Mary.

"Few eyes," says Sir Thomas Browne, "have escaped the picture of a mermaid with a woman's head above and a fish's extremity below." In those old days when reading and writing were rare accomplishments, pictured signboards served to give "a local habitation and a name" to hostelries and other places of business and resort. Among the most celebrated of the old London taverns bearing this sign,* that in Bread Street stands foremost.

* The sign was also used by printers : John Rastall, brother-in-law to Sir Thomas More, " emprynted in the

We find this " Mermayde " mentioned as early as 1464. In 1603 Sir Walter Raleigh established a literary club in this house, and here Shakespeare, Ben Jonson, and the choice intellectual spirits of the time used to meet, and there took place those wit combats which Beaumont has commemorated and Fuller described. It is frequently alluded to by Beaumont and Fletcher in their comedies, but best known is that quotation from a letter of Beaumont to Ben Jonson :

> " What things have we seen
> Done at the Mermaid ? heard words that have been
> So nimble and so full of subtle flame,
> As if that any one from whence they came
> Had meant to put his whole wit in a jest,
> And had resolved to live a fool the rest
> Of his dull life ; then when there had been thrown
> Wit able enough to justify the town
> For three days past ; wit that might warrant be
> For the whole city to talk foolishly,
> Till that were cancell'd ; and when that was gone,
> We left an air behind us, which alone
> Was able to make the next two companies
> (Right witty, though but downright fools) more wise."

Cheapesyde at the Sygne of the Mermayde ; next to Powls-gate in 1572." Henry Binnemann, the Queen's printer, dedicated a work to Sir Thomas Gresham, in 1576, at the sign of the Mermaid, Knightrider Street. A representation of the creature was generally prefixed to his books.— " History of Sign-boards," p. 227.

The Dolphin of Legend and of Heraldry

"... *his delights*
Were dolphin-like ; they showed his back above
The element they lived in."
"Anthony and Cleopatra," Act v. sc. 2.

As the Lion is the king of beasts, the Eagle the king
of birds, so in similar heraldic sense the Dolphin is
king of fishes. His position in legend is probably
due to his being one of the biggest and boldest
creatures of the sea that passed the Pillars of Hercules
into the Mediterranean Sea. Pliny (Book ix. ch. 8)
calls it " The swiftest of all other living creatures
whatsoever, and not of sea fish only, is the dolphin ;
quicker than any fowle, swifter than the arrow shot
from a bow."

The dolphin, of which there are several varieties,

enjoys a pretty wide geographical distribution, being found in the Arctic seas, the Atlantic Ocean, and indeed of all seas.   It was well known to the ancients and furnished the theme of many a fabulous story.

The common dolphin (*Delphinus Delphis*) the true *hieros ichthus*, is only rarely met with on the British coast.   Its length is usually seven or eight feet, though some specimens have been found to

The Dolphin.

measure ten feet.   Its back is almost straight, or only slightly elevated; its colour is dusky black above and whitish beneath.   Its pectorals or flappers, which are placed low in the sides, are well developed, and a dorsal fin, which is somewhat short, is much elevated. Its tail is broad and notched in the centre and expanded horizontally—not vertically as in most other fishes—by the help of which it makes its peculiar leaps over the surface of the water and at the same time takes its breath.

Unlike its near relatives the porpoises, who haunt the coast, dolphins live far out at sea, and are generally mistaken for porpoises.   The long-snouted dolphin feeds on pelagic fishes.   The short-nosed porpoise likes salmon and mackerel, robs the fishermen's nets, and even burrows in the sand in search of odds and ends.   The dolphin is the sea-goose.

The porpoise is the sea-pig ; he is the *porc-poisson*, the *porc-pois*, or sea-hog.

The convex snout of the dolphin is separated from the forehead by a deep furrow ; the muzzle is greatly extended, compressed, and much attenuated especially towards the apex, where it terminates in a rather sharp-pointed beak. The French name *bec d'oie*, from the great projection of its nose or beak, has led to its adoption in the arms of English families of the name of Beck. The dolphin is an elegant and swift swimmer, and capable of overtaking the swiftest of the finny tribe. Because the creature is noted for its swiftness it has been adopted in the arms of Fleet.

The dolphin is able to hold his own against nearly all others of his size and weight, and even some of the larger cetaceans only come off second best in an encounter with the dolphin. He is voracious, gluttonous, and ever on the look out for something to turn up, hunting his prey with great persistency and devouring it with avidity. He has been not inaptly styled " the plunderer of the deep."

The destructive character of the dolphin amongst the various tribes of fish is not lessened when we examine its formidable jaws studded with an immense number of interlocking teeth. Notwithstanding its rapacious habits and the variety of its diet it was in England formerly regarded as a royal fish, and its flesh held in high estimation. Old chroniclers have frequent entries of dolphins being caught in the Thames, thus : " 3 Henry V.—Seven dolphins came up the Thames, whereof four were taken." "14th Richard II.—On Christmas Day one was taken at London Bridge, being ten feet long, and a monstrous grown fish." (Delalune's " Present State of London," 1681.) The early fathers of the Church deemed " all fish that swam in the sea " ; the dolphin was therefore eaten in Lent. He is, however, a mammal, not a fish, and though an air-breathing creature he lives and dies in the ocean. But one is brought forth at a birth, and between the old and young of their kind, as in the case of all marine animals, a strong affection exists.

Travellers' tales are notoriously hard of belief, and must be taken *cum grano salis*. We learn from Sir Thomas Herbert, an early voyager, that when he was on the coast of Sanquehar, a large kingdom on the east side of the Cape of Good Hope, he " saw there great numbers of dolphins," of which he says : " They much affect the company of men, and are nourished like men ; they are always constant to their mates, tenderly affected to their parents, feeding and defending them against hungry fishes when they are old," and much more information equally astonishing.

A story is related of a man who once went to a mufti and asked him whether the flesh of the sea-pig (the dolphin) was lawful food. Without any hesitation the mufti declared that pig's flesh was unlawful at all times and under all circumstances. Some time after another person submitted the question to the same authority, whether the *fish* of the sea, called the sea-

R

pig, was lawful food. The mufti replied : " Fish is
lawful food by whatever name it may be called."

CLASSIC FABLE and MEDIÆVAL LEGEND have shed
a halo of romantic interest around the dolphin which
cleaves to it even to the present hour ; the rare
event of a dolphin being caught in British waters
revives with a thrill all the old-world stories and historic associations of this famous fish as if it were a
veritable relic of the golden age. The dolphin of
fact we have found to be quite a different creature
from what he is pictured by the ancients. The
mariner may be engulfed by " the yawning, dashing,
furious sea," but no generous dolphin now watches
with tender eye, solicitous for his safety, nor offers his
ready back to speed him to the shore.

The dolphin of our modern poets and sailors—
the swift swimmer that leaps after the flying-fish and
frolics in front of the vessel's prow until he is caught
by the glittering tin—is the *Coryphæna hippurus*, the
species famed for its changing tints when taken from
the water. During a calm, these fishes, when swimming about a ship, appear of a brilliant blue or purple,
shining with a metallic lustre in every change of re-
flected light. On being captured and brought on deck,
the variety of these tints is very beautiful. The bright
purple and golden yellow hues change to brilliant
silver, varying back again into the original colours,
purple and gold. This alteration of tints continues
for some time, diminishing in intensity, and at last
settles down into a dull leaden hue. The iridescent

lines which play along its elegant curves as he lies on deck has awakened the enthusiasm of many a writer. Byron tells us in a beautiful simile :

> " Parting day
> Dies like the dolphin, whom each pang imbues
> With a new lustre, as it gasps away,
> The last still loveliest, till 'tis gone—and all is grey."

It is needless to say that the legendary dolphin is not to be confounded with the gay and graceful *coryphæna* to whom alone belong those rainbow flashes of colour in dying. The common dolphin (*Delphinus delphis*) is dark on the back and satiny

Dolphin of classic art.

white beneath but not even in the agonies of death does he change colour, though like all dead things the body becomes slightly phosphorescent during decomposition. There are two curious fresh water dolphins, the Sooloo of the Ganges and the Inia of the Amazon, which form the connecting-link between the herbaceous and carnivorous cetacea.

The dolphin (δελφίν) may be considered an accessory symbol of Apollo, who, as we read in the Homeric hymns, once took the form of a dolphin when he guided the Cretan ship to Crissa, whence, after commanding the crew to burn the ship and erect an altar to him as Apollo Delphinios, he led them to

Delphi, and appointed them to be the first priests of his temple.

The dolphin is the most classic of fishes, the favourite of Apollo, and sacred to that bright divinity, deriving his name from the oracular Delphi, that mysterious spot, "the earth's umbilicus," the very centre of the world, Delphi or Delphos, a town in Phocis, famous for its oracle in the Temple of Apollo, upon the walls of which were sculptured the *Helios ichthus*, Apollo's fish.

In the legend of Tarento, Phalantus, heading the Patheniæ, was driven from Sparta and shipwrecked off the coast of Italy, and escaped on a friendly dolphin's back to Tarentum. We learn from Aristotle that the youthful figure seated on the dolphin, which is the most common type on the coins of this city, was intended for Taras, a son of Poseidon, from whom the city is said to have derived its name.

The dolphins, "the arrows of the sea," were the great carriers of ancient times. Not only did they bear the Nereides safely on their backs, but Arion, the sweet singer, when forced to leap into the sea to escape the mariners who would have murdered him, had previously so charmed the dolphins by his playing that they gathered round the ship and one of them bore Arion safely to Tænarus, whilst the musician

> "with harmonious strains
> Requites his bearer for his friendly pains."

The classic myth of Arion and the dolphin, like

many other pagan fictions, was invested by the early Christians with an entirely different significa- tion, and in the sculptures and frescoes of the catacombs and other symbolic representations of the Christian converts, the frequent introduction of the dolphin " points not to the deliverer of Arion, but to Him who through the waters of baptism opens to mankind the paths of deliverance, causing them to so pass the waves of this troublesome world that finally they may come to the land of everlasting life."

The poet Licophron says Ulysses bore a dolphin on his shield, on the pommel of his sword, as well as on his ring, in commemoration of the extraordinary escape of his son Telemachus, who when young fell into the sea and was taken up by a dolphin and safely brought on shore. Pliny and others relate a story of one of these fishes which frequented the Lake Lucrin : " A boy who went every day to school from Baia to Puzzoli used to feed this dolphin with bread, and it became at last so familiar with the boy that it carried him often on its back over the bay."

The dolphins were early symbols on the coins of Ægina, and though abandoned for a time were after- wards resumed ; and they appear upon later and well-known coins of that State accompanied by the wolf and other national devices. Argos had anciently two dolphins ; Syracuse, a winged sea-dog, a dolphin, &c. ; Teneos (Cyclades) two dolphins and a trident. The dolphin and trident figures also upon coins of the ancient city of Byzantium, signifying probably the sovereignty of the seas. It is even figured by the ancients as a constellation in the heraldry of the heavens. In botany it lives in larkspurs called delphiniums, from their curious petals and the slender segments of their leaves.

Coin of Ægina.

The dolphin and anchor is a famous historic symbol. Titus, Emperor of Rome, took the device of a dolphin twisted round an anchor, to imply, like the emblem of Augustus, the medium between haste and slowness, the anchor being the symbol of delay, as it is also of firmness and security, while the dolphin is the swiftest of fish. This device appears also upon the coins of Vespasian, the father of Titus. The anchor was also used as a signet ring by Seleneus, King of Syria. The dolphin and anchor was also used, with the motto "Festina lente" ("Hasten slowly"), by the Emperor Adolphus of Nassau, and by Admiral Chabot. The family of Onslow bear the same for crest and motto.

Aldus Manutius, the celebrated Venetian printer, adopted this well-known device from a silver medal presented to him by Cardinal Bembo, with the motto in Greek " hasten slowly." Camerarius describes this sign in his book of symbols "to represent that maturity in business which is the medium between too great haste and slowness." " When violent winds disturb the sea the anchor is cast by seamen, the dolphin

winds herself round it out of a particular love for
mankind, and directs it as with a human intellect so
that it may more
safely take hold of
the ground ; for
dolphins have this
peculiar property that
they can, as it were,
foretell storms. The
anchor then signifies
a stay and security
whilst the dolphin is
a hieroglyphic for
philanthropy and
safety."

*Aldus
Printer*

*Venice.
A.D. 1490 1563.*

This sign was after-
wards adopted by William Pickering, a worthy
" Discipulus Aldi " as he styles himself. Sir Eger-
ton Bridges has some verses upon it, amongst which
occur the following :

" Would thou still be safely landed,
On the Aldine anchor ride ;
Never yet was vessel stranded,
With the dolphin by its side.

.   .   .   .   .

" Nor time nor envy shall ever canker,
The sign which is my lasting pride ;
Joy then to the Aldus anchor
And the dolphin at its side.

" To the dolphin as we're drinking,
    Life and health and joy we send ;
A poet once he saved from sinking,
    And still he lives the poet's friend."

The dolphin was the insignia of the Eastern Empire
—the Empire of Constantinople. The Courteneys,
a noble Devonshire family, still bear the dolphin as
crest and badge, and the melancholy motto, " Ubi
lapsus ? Quid feci ? " (" Whither have I fallen ?
What have I done ? "), " a touching allusion," says
Miss Millington (" Heraldry in History and
Romance"), " to the misfortunes of their race, three
of whom filled the imperial throne of Constantinople
during the time that city was in possession of the
Latins after the siege of 1204. Expelled at length by
the Greeks, Baldwin, the last of the three, wandered
from Court to Court throughout Europe vainly
seeking aid to replace him upon the throne."

A branch of the imperial Courteneys settled in
England during the reign of Henry II., and their
descendants were among the principal Barons of the
realm. Three Earls of Courteney perished on the
scaffold during the Wars of the Roses ; the family
was restored to favour by Henry VII. Another
Courteney, the Marquis of Exeter, became first the
favourite, and subsequently the victim of the brutal
tyrant Henry VIII. His son Edward, after being
long a prisoner in the tower, ended his days in exile,
and the family estates passed into other hands.

Sir William Courteney, of Powderham Castle,

Devon (*temp*. Edw. IV.), bore emblazoned on his standard three dolphins in reference to the purple of three Emperors.

The Arms of Peter Courteney, Bishop of Exeter, 1478, is still to be seen in the episcopal palace environed with the dolphins of Constantinople.

The Dauphin of France

In France the bearing of the dolphin was exclusively restricted to the Dauphin or heir to the throne of the kingdom. Brydson mentions that one of the first of the troubadours was called the Dauphin, or Knight of the Dolphin, from bearing that figure on his shield, adding that "the name in his successors became a title of sovereign dignity."

Banner of the Dauphin.

The title "Dauphin," borne by the eldest son and heir-apparent of the kings of France under the Valois and Bourbon dynasties, originated in the Dauphins of Viennois, sovereigns of the province of Dauphiné. Guy VIII., Count of Vienne, was the first so styled. The title descended in the family till 1349, when

Humbert II., *de la Tour de Pisa*, sold his seigneurie, called the Dauphiné, to Philippe VI. (de Valois), on condition that the heir of France assumed the title of "Le Dauphin." The first French prince so called was Jean, who succeeded Philippe ; and the last was the Duc d'Angoulême, son of Charles X., who renounced the title in 1830. In 1601, when Louis XIII. was born, there had not been a Dauphin since Francis II. (the husband of Mary, Queen of Scots)—eighty-four years. The province of Dauphiné sent a deputation to Fontainebleau, headed by the Archbishop of Vienne, to recognise the infant as their sovereign, and make him a present of an entire service of richly chased plate with various figures of dolphins, estimated at 12,000 crowns.

GRAND DAUPHIN.—Louis, duc de Bourgogne, eldest son of Louis XIV., for whom was published the edition of the Latin classics entitled " Ad usum Delphini" (1661–1711).

SECOND, OR LITTLE DAUPHIN.—Louis, son of the Grand Dauphin (1682–1712).

Shakespeare, by an anachronism of a hundred years, introduced into King John

"Lewis, the Dauphin and the heir of France."

Mary Queen of Scots bore the title on her marriage in 1558 to the Dauphin, afterwards Francis II., and styled by her adherents :

"Mary, Queen, and Dolphiness of Fraunce,
The nobillest lady in earth."

The Heraldic Dolphin

THE heraldic dolphin, as usually represented by modern heralds, is an ornamental monstrosity bearing

but slight resemblance to the natural form of this celebrated historic marine symbol ; a nearer resemblance to the natural shape is decidedly preferable. Some of the early heraldic representations, though a little crude, are very characteristic and thoroughly heraldic in treatment, though at the same time very unlike the real dolphin.

In its series of leaps out of the water the dolphin appears with high arched back, just as we see it represented in antique works ; its

Example—Dolphin embowed.

natural shape, however, is straight, the back being but slightly curved. The broad tail paddle being placed in a horizontal position necessitates an up and down stroke, which makes their swimming to appear a series of leaps and divings.   Like its near relative the porpoise, it is an air-breathing animal ; its apparent gambollings on the water may, therefore, be more truly attributed to its breathing and blowing whilst in pursuit of its prey.

The Dolphin is generally, if not always, depicted in heraldry *embowed*, that is, having its back greatly incurvated.   In blazon the word *Dolphin*, alone, implies that its natural position, *naiant* (swimming) and embowed, is understood, but for the sake of accuracy it is better always to give the description in full, as a doubt may arise as to the omission of a word indicating its position.

Torqued, torquend, torgant, or *targant*, from the Latin *torquere*, to twist, are old terms for embowed, or bowed embowed, bent in the form of the letter S, turning contrary ways at each bending ; applicable also to serpents.

Hauriant, from the Latin *ab hauriendo*, is a term applied to fishes generally when placed in an upright position or *in pale*, as if putting the head above water to get air.

Hauriant   Urinant   Naiant   Torqued

Shell-fish are blazoned *erect* or *upright*, the term
hauriant being only applicable to fishes with scales
and fins.

Urinant (from the Latin *urino*, to duck or dive
under water) signifies borne with the head downwards and the tail erect, the reverse position of
hauriant.

Two dolphins are occasionally borne together,
sometimes endorsed, or back to back ; sometimes
respecting each other.

As signifying the conquest of the sea, it appears
in the shields of many seaport cities. It figures on
the well-known bearings of the towns of Brighton,
Dunkirk, Poole, &c.

The Dolphin appears in English heraldry as early
as the middle of the thirteenth century. In a roll of
arms of that date, a dolphin is given as the coat of
Gile de Fiseburn.

" The Godolphins of Helston," says Miss Millington, " who had estates in that part of the kingdom
(Cornwall) at the time of the Conquest, bore *argent
three dolphins embowed, sable*." Similar arms are borne
by many English families.

The Godolphins, Franklins, Franklands, Frenches,
Fishers and Kennedys, in many of their branches,
bear the dolphin fish as their crest.

.A man playing the harp on a dolphin is the
heraldic cognisance of the Walterton family.

Sea-horse naiant.

The Sea-horse

" His sea-horses did seem to snort amain
And from their nostrils blow the fiery stream
That made the sparkling waves to smoke again
And flame with gold ; but the white foam cream
Did shine with silver, and shoot forth his beam."
SPENSER'S *Faerie Queen.*
(Procession of the Sea Divinities.)

THE steeds of Neptune are favourite subjects in
ancient poetry and art in the triumphs and processions
of the marine deities, drawing the chariot of the sea-
god in its progress through the waves. The imaginative Greeks pictured to themselves the horses of
Poseidon in the rolling and bounding waves as they
pursue each other in haste towards the shore, " curling
their monstrous heads." This may seem to account
for the constant and close connection between the
god and the horse. The origin of the horse is

ascribed to the contest between Poseidon and Athenæ
as to who should make to mankind the most useful
present ; Neptune created the horse, Minerva the
olive-tree.

The city of Lampsacus, in Mysia, founded by the
Phoceans, adopted the winged sea-horse as their
monetary type, in
allusion to the fleet-
ness of their vessels.
Others of the mari-
time States of Greece
also adopted the sea-
horse upon their coins.

A coin of the cele-
brated Pyrrhus, King
of Epirus (slain B.C.
272), the knight-
errant of ancient
heroes, represents the
head of Achilles, the
reputed ancestor of

Sea-horse erect.

Pyrrhus, on one side, and the Nereid, Thetis, the
mother of Achilles, on the sea-horse on the reverse.
Thetis carries the arms forged by Vulcan for Achilles,
in allusion to the succour brought by Pyrrhus to
the Italian Greeks against the barbarians, as the rising
Romans were termed by them.

In Gibbon's " Decline and Fall of the Roman
Empire," we find a reference to a veritable sea-horse,
if we may believe our authority.   John Sobieski, the

victorious King of Poland, in his letters to his wife, when he raised the memorable siege of Vienna and delivered Europe for ever from the incursions of the Turks, describes to her how, in the tent of Mustapha, he found the great standard of the Turks, "*made of the hair of the sea-horse* (?) *wrought with a needle and embroidered with Arabic figures*." It was afterwards hung up by the order of the Emperor in the Cathedral of St. Stephens, "where," adds the historian, "*I have seen it*."

The coast of Naples is celebrated for the production of a small fish in great repute with mothers who nurse their offspring; among its other virtues it is said to cure the bite of a mad dog. It is about four to six inches in length, and has a head resembling that of a horse, terminating in a dragon's tail. This is the tiny hippocampus of our public aquariums. The Neapolitans call them "cavalli-marini," which was once ingeniously translated by a learned English traveller as "horse marines."

This fabulous marine creature in heraldry is compounded of the fore quarters of a horse with webbed paws, and the hinder part of a fish or dolphin. A scalloped fin is continued down the neck and back in place of a mane. It is frequently, though erroneously, to be seen depicted with the flowing mane of a horse; wings are also sometimes added to it, both of which, it is needless to say, are wrong, unless specially mentioned in the blazon.

The Westenras (Baron Rossmore), descended from

the family of Van Wassenhaer of Wassenburg, were of great antiquity in Holland, and they bore the augmentation of the sea-horse in reference to the valour and intrepidity of an ancestor, who, during the

Arms of the city of Belfast.
The sinister supporter and crest are Sea-horses.

Duke of Alva's campaign, was actively employed against the enemies of his country and undertook at great risk to swim across an arm of the sea with important despatches to his besieged countrymen.

The Sea-horse is of very frequent use in armory, and usually has reference to meritorious actions performed at sea. It is also borne by many seaport towns

S

in allusion to the trade and commerce of the port, as in the arms of the city of Belfast.

Cromwell, Protector, bore as supporters a lion of England and a sea-horse, probably to denote his protectorship of the sea, as of the land.

Bossewell (" Works of Armorie," 1589), in his peculiar mixture of English and Latin, gives a quaint description of the animal : " This water-horse of the sea is called a hippotame, for that he is like an horse in back, mayne, and neying : rostro resupinato a primis dentibus : cauda tortuosa, ungulis binis. He abideth in the waters on the day, and eateth corn by night et hunc Nilus gignit." The latter may be classed with those fantastic ornamental forms frequently employed in fountains and waterworks, such as the *Ichthyocentaur*, *i.e.*, a combination of man and horse, or the centaur with a fish's extremity.

Sea=lion

or *Lion poisson*, a mythical sea-creature, frequently used in heraldry as an emblem of bold actions achieved on the ocean in the country's service. It is depicted as the fore part of a lion with webbed feet, the hinder part ending in a fish's tail.

Two such animals support the arms of Viscount Falmouth.

The Earl of Howth has for supporters *a sea-lion*

argent, and a mermaid, proper. The crest also is a sea-lion.

The crest of Duckworth is *a tower, the battlements partly demolished, from the top flames issuant proper; on the sinister side a sea-lion erect azure, pressing against the tower.*

Silvestre. — *Argent, a sea-lion couchant azure, crowned armed and langued gules.*

Sea-lion erect.

When the sea-lion or other compounded creature of this kind is erect, it should be clearly blazoned as " a sea-lion erect on his tail," to distinguish it from naiant, the swimming position natural to it.

Sea=dog

is depicted like a talbot in shape, but with the tail like that of a beaver, the feet webbed and the whole body scaled like a fish, a scalloped fin continued along the back from the head to the tail.

Baron Stourton has two such beasts, sable, scaled or, for his supporters.

The crest of Sir H. Delves Broughton.—*A sea-dog's head gules, eared and finned argent.*

The SEA-BULL, SEA-WOLF, SEA-BEAR, SEA-CAT, SEA-DRAGON, etc., when they occur in heraldry, are all depicted as having the anterior portions of their bodies in the forms which their several names denote ; but, like the sea-lion and sea-horse, they have fishes tails and webbed paws.

Sea-dog rampant.

In conclusion, having, as far as possible, given the *raison d'être* of each, and traced the life-history and characteristics of the many strange and fantastic creatures in our symbolic menagerie, it only remains to express the hope that the information contained in this volume may be found both interesting and useful, as without some such knowledge there can be little or no intelligent understanding of the proper treatment of the forms of these mythical and symbolic beings. The suggestive illustrations, while giving the recognised forms of each, leaves to the artist free scope to adopt his own style of art treatment, whether purely heraldic or merely decorative.